Healing

MORE THAN A THEORY

Becky Combee

HEALING: MORE THAN A THEORY
   By Becky Combee
Published by Becky Combee Ministries, Inc.
P.O. Box 3283
Lakeland, FL 33802-3283
Beckycombeeministries.com

ISBN-13: 978-0-9832783-5-1
ISBN-10: 0-9832783-5-0

Cover by Suzanne D. Williams.

Unless otherwise noted, all Scripture references were taken from the King James Version of the Bible.

Scripture notations marked AMP were taken from the Amplified® Bible, Copyright © 1954, 1958, 1962, 1964, 1965, 1987 by The Lockman Foundation. Used by permission. <http://www.lockman.org>.

Scripture notations marked CEV were taken from the Contemporary English Version Copyright © 1991, 1992, 1995 by American Bible Society, Used by Permission.

Definitions marked MW were taken from Merriam-Webster.com. Accessed 18 August 2014.

Definitions marked "Webster's" were taken from Webster's 1828 Dictionary, <http://www.e-sword.net> Accessed 18 August 2014.

References marked Barnes were taken from Albert Barnes' Notes on the Bible, <http://www.e-sword.net> Accessed 18 August 2014.

References marked Clarke were taken from Adam Clarke's Commentary on the Bible, <http://www.e-sword.net> Accessed 18 August 2014.

References marked Easton were taken from Easton's Bible Dictionary, <http://www.e-sword.net> Accessed 18 August 2014.

References marked Jewish Enc. were taken from the Jewish Encylopedia <http://www.jewishencyclopedia.com/articles/8692-job> Accessed 18 August 2014.

References marked McCrossan are from T.J. McCrossan, Bodily Healing and the Atonement, Re-Edited by Dr. Roy Hicks and Dr. Kenneth E. Hagin, 2d ed., First printing, (Oklahoma: RHEMA Bible Church AKA Kenneth Hagin Ministries, Inc. 1982).

The Song1 reference comes from "'Whosoever' Meaneth Me" by James E. McConnell, 1910.

The Vines1 reference can be found at Reconcile,Reconciliation/A.Verbs/1.Katallasso in Vine, W.E., M.A., Vine's Expository Dictionary of New Testament Words, Unabridged ed. (McLean, Va.: MacDonald Publishing Company).

TABLE OF CONTENTS

SECTION FOUR

No More Obstacles

DEDICATION

Once again, I dedicate another book to the tireless and unfailing work of our daughter, Suzanne. Her expertise is of such great value that it cannot be overstated or exaggerated. Dad and I love you!

I am also eternally grateful for the unceasing prayers of our five faithful friends. Together, you have brought heaven to our hearts. Thank you, Carol, Korita, Mary Lynn, Susan, and Vicki. You are treasured!!

Becky Combee

INTRODUCTION

I have studied divine healing from the Word of God and the great masters of faith for over three decades, and of all the messages that I have absorbed, one continues to speak to me. Believe it or not, it is on death.

I suppose, most of us are afraid of dying. We want to live forever and ever and ever, AND we will. But there will be a day of transition, of relocation through the door of death. Every man is an eternal spirit-being made in the image and likeness of God. Through sin, we are separated from God, our Creator, and united with Satan. But God loved us and sent Jesus to be our Savior. Through Jesus' death and resurrection, our sins are remitted, God becomes our Father, and heaven is our home. What wonderful news!

However, if we do not receive Christ as Savior and Lord, heaven is not home. We remain in Satan's kingdom, and his nature rules our lives. The Scripture is very clear. Jesus said to the Jews, "Ye are of your father the devil."[1] This is true for all who reject God's bountiful provision through Jesus Christ.

Both saint and sinner will pass from this life into the future they have chosen. Physical death comes to all. Yet in spite of this inevitability and the glorious future

---

[1] Jn 8:44

prepared for every Christian, fear of death often dominates the hearts and minds of God's children. This fear of death is a hindrance to health and healing.

> Although God has spoken, "I am the Lord that healeth thee,"[2] usually when medical science unveils a potential sickness or disease, fear easily dominates our mind and emotions. The Word from God is too far removed, even from the hearts of Christians, and fails to be of comfort.

So, what was it about a lesson on death that calmed my fears and set me free? It was these two simple words, **SO WHAT**. These words are significant because they embrace several powerful truths. First, sickness does not eliminate my eternal destiny, and it cannot separate us from our God. Secondly, sickness does not alter God's healing word or His promise of long life.

The Word of the Lord says:

With long life will I satisfy him.[3]

---

[2] Ex 15:26
[3] Ps 91:16

God wants us to live a long time. He said so. It is not hard to face sickness and say SO WHAT when we understand these truths.

What then about those precious Christians that have died prematurely? The apostle Paul gives God's glorious answer, "To die is gain."[4] Oh, what marvelous words of comfort! When the door of death closes to earth's captivity, the gates of heaven open to the presence of God our Father and Jesus our Lord.

In His presence, "There shall be no more death, neither sorrow, nor crying, neither shall there be any more pain."[5]

Yet I cannot and I will not allow disease to shorten my life. I am God's ambassador. I am commissioned to "go into my world" with the good news that Jesus is Lord. I can, without fear of death, cherish every minute of time laboring with God.[6]

Therefore, I say to death, SO WHAT.

---

4 Php 1:21
5 Rev 21:4
6 Mk 16:15, author's paraphrase

I will "fight a good fight and finish my course."[7] I will run with God every mile of the way and finish the job God has assigned to me. When sickness attacks my body, I will stand with the Word of God in my heart and in my mouth. God will perform His Word!

This is why we have written this book. We want everyone to understand God's healing Word and enjoy the fullness of His provision. He is the Lord, our healer.

Becky Combee

---

[7] 2Ti 4:7, author's paraphrase

SECTION 1

NO MORE DOUBT

Then said Jesus to those Jews which believed on him, If ye continue in my word, then are ye my disciples indeed; And ye shall know the truth, and the truth shall make you free (Jn 8:31-32).

CHAPTER 1

THREE WORDS

Religion today often makes disease an endowment of heaven used for divine purpose. Yet when our body is wracked with pain, we don't want to suffer. Instead, we actively seek relief. We want to be free. Disease simply is not a relaxing experience.

According to the Word of God, sickness is the bondage and oppression of Satan. It is not the work of our heavenly Father's compassionate heart or a reflection of His goodness. In fact, the Word of God declares that God, our Father, gives good and perfect gifts.[1] Certainly, sickness is NOT a good and perfect gift! **Sickness is an enemy – a thief!**

Our heavenly Father will not oppress us or bind us with disease. He never uses sickness to steal our comfort, our time, or our finances. He does not challenge our lives with the curse of sickness to glorify Himself or to teach us a valuable lesson.

After many years of instructing sick people, I can assure you they are very poor students. It is difficult and even impossible to focus on God's Word when your

---

[1] Jas 1:17

body is tormented by disease. Sickness is a very ineffective teacher, and after all, the Holy Spirit is our Teacher.[2]

Oh, how great it is to be well! When we are well—healed and made whole—God is glorified. The Scripture consistently declares this truth. After the man with palsy was healed, the multitudes marveled and glorified God.[3] The women with a spirit of infirmity also glorified God after she was healed.[4] The Scripture records:

When they saw the dumb to speak, the maimed to be whole, the lame to walk, and the blind to see ... they glorified the God of Israel.[5]

Healing always glorifies God!

A CURSE

Certainly, God's Word is true, and it says disease is a curse, not a blessing. According to the American Dictionary of the English Language, a blessing is "any means of happiness," and "that which promotes

---

[2] Jn 14:26
[3] Mt 9:8
[4] Lk 13:13
[5] Mt 15:31

temporal prosperity and welfare."[6] A curse vexes, harasses, and torments us.[7] With every curse, there is the expectation of pain and suffering. We do not expect a "curse" to provide happiness and prosperity.

The curse of sickness is as persistent as a child begging for permission to leave home just before dinner time. Following you from room to room, he pleads, "Can I go to Mark's house? Please? I'll be right back. Please, let me go."

In like manner, sickness unrelentingly attacks our bodies. It speaks continually to the mind saying, "Do you feel that? Can you sense that? You're really, really sick." Then it makes the grand announcement, "You may not get well. You probably will die."

Sickness is a curse!

In Deuteronomy 28:15-68, God enumerates the curses that would overtake His people if His commandments were broken. There are a number of diseases listed here and although we may not recognize them by these archaic names, we are sure each one is a curse. In verse 22, God mentions consumption, fever, inflammation, and extreme burning. In verse 27, we read about botch, emerods, scab and itch. God also lists mental distress described as madness, blindness, and

---

6 Webster's 1828
7 Webster's 1959

astonishment of heart. No human malady is excluded because verse 61 says "every sickness and every plague" will destroy us.

Each of these diseases harasses us, torments and vexes us. Over and over again, they invade our lives proving the truth of God's Word. It declares that they are a curse, and a curse is never a blessing!

BONDAGE

In Luke 13, Jesus healed a woman whose body had been bowed over for eighteen years. When He laid His hands on her, immediately she stood up straight. However, the ruler of the synagogue was indignant because Jesus healed her on the Sabbath. Jesus response to this religious adversary was:

Ought not this woman, being a daughter of Abraham, whom Satan hath bound, lo, these eighteen years, be loosed from this bond on the Sabbath day?[8]

There are two very enlightening facts in Jesus' answer. First, she was bound by disease. When anything

---

[8] Lk 13:16

is bound, it is tied and restricted. A policeman binds or handcuffs suspected criminals before he locks them in his car to transport them to a secure facility. They are not free! When they are later granted a court appearance or a trial, they are again handcuffed and often their feet are chained. Then if they are convicted of a crime, they are confined to a prison facility. In this facility, they are constantly guarded and every activity is dictated by those in authority.

> *Sickness always binds us and steals our freedom.*

It dominates our life, restricting our activities and altering our schedules. It commands us, saying, 'You can't go to work today. You have to stay in bed and you can't eat anything."

Yet the Word of God declares:

Ye shall know the truth, and the truth shall make you free.[9]

But there isn't any freedom or liberty in disease. Disease binds, tie, and restricts.

---

[9] Jn 8:32

Furthermore, this bondage is orchestrated by Satan. In Luke 13:16, Jesus testified to this fact saying the woman with a spirit of infirmity was bound by the devil. **The devil is the enemy that holds us captive.** Our magnificent Father certainly does not imprison His people, not by ignorance, not by poverty, and certainly not by disease.

> *Sickness is never a joint venture between Satan and God.*

Satan invades our lives with disease and calamity, but Jesus is our Healer. In Him, we are free.

OPPRESSION

In Acts 10:38, the apostle Peter also identifies Satan as the author of sickness and disease.

Here, he declares:

> *How God anointed Jesus of Nazareth with the Holy Ghost and with power: who went about doing good, and*

healing all that were oppressed of the devil.[10]

This proves that **sickness is an oppression that comes from Satan**, not from our great and marvelous Father.

According to Webster's New Collegiate dictionary, the word *oppression* means to crush or burden by abuse of power or authority. This fitting description of Satan's work is confirmed in the New International Version.

[Jesus] went around doing good and healing all who were under the power of the devil.

The Knox Translation says Jesus was:

...curing all those who were under the devil's tyranny.

Jesus routed this work of Satan by the power of the

---

[10] Act 10:38

Holy Spirit. He healed every sickness and every disease among the people, pouring out heaven's mercy on the sick. [11] With the anointing of heaven, He set the oppressed free. Then by His death on the cross, He spoiled Satan, disarming him and stripping him of his power. [12]

Now, Satan cannot successfully oppress our bodies and our minds. He cannot conquer or bind us with the curse of sickness because he was defeated by the risen Christ. **Boldly, we declare, "Jesus has destroyed the works of Satan, and I am free. Healing is mine."** Satan and sickness must bow their knee because Jesus is my Lord and My Physician. AMEN!

---

[11] Mt 9:35
[12] Col 2:15

CHAPTER 2

FROM SIN TO SICKNESS

After God created the world, Satan appeared in the Garden of Eden disguised as a serpent –cunning and deceitful. As the enemy of man and the enemy of God, his first self-appointed task was to question the instructions that God had given Adam. He asked Eve:

What is this command God has given you, not to eat the fruit of any tree in the garden?[1]

Eve replied:

We may eat of the fruit of the trees of the garden: But of the fruit of the tree which is in the midst of the garden, God hath said, Ye shall not eat of it, neither shall ye touch it, lest ye die.[2]

Directly contradicting Almighty God, Satan

---

[1] Ge 3:1 Knox
[2] Ge 3:2-3

responded, "Ye shall not surely die," and then he promised Eve if she and Adam ate the forbidden fruit they would be like gods, knowing good and evil.[3]

Oh, what deception! Subtly, he enticed Eve to sin, and, of course, Adam also. This sin opened their eyes to good and evil just as Satan had promised. However, instead of the godly promotion they had expected, they were trapped by evil, unable to recover from its devastating effects.

Before Satan's deception, Adam and Eve walked in the glory of God, so dominated by God's presence that they didn't know they were naked.[4] They saw life with the eyes of their spirit, not through their flesh and physical senses. However, **after they sinned, their vision changed**, and they saw through the eyes of evil. What Satan promised as wonderful, even glorious, was devastating. Satan's words came to pass; his lie prospered, but it wasn't wonderful.

SIN AND DEATH

This great change in Adam and Eve's life is easier to understand if we grasp the scriptural concept of death. Three kinds of death dominate the Word of God:

> *Spiritual death, physical death, and eternal death (also called the second death).*

---

[3] Ge 3:4-5
[4] Ge 2:25

Often, we think only in terms of physical death, defining it in the broadest of generalities, "to cease to exist." But no man ceases to exist. After physical death, everyone lives somewhere, either in heaven or in hell, either with the Lord or in the place of punishment. Man cannot cease to exist because he is a spirit being and his spirit is eternal.

I believe death is more correctly defined as separation. Physical death is separation from earth's reality, separation from friends and family, and most of all, the separation of man's spirit from his physical body. Spiritual death is separation from God and His kingdom because of sin. Through sin we embrace the nature of Satan and are plunged into his kingdom.

> *If we do not choose Jesus as our Savior and Lord, we inherit the place of permanent separation from God, the lake of fire, which is called eternal death.*[5]

Spiritual death became the plight of Adam and Eve. Before Adam and Eve's sin, God warned Adam that THE DAY he ate of the tree of the knowledge of good an evil he would die.[6] We know this did not mean physical death because Adam lived over 800 years after he

---

[5] Rev 20:6,14
[6] Ge 2:17

sinned.[7] Instead, **the consequence of Adam and Eve's sin and disobedience was spiritual death**. Because of sin, they died spiritually and were separated from God. Then when God came to walk with them in the garden, they hid from His presence. They had been captured by the world of evil and for the first time were afraid.

THE CURSE OF SIN

Fear was not the only consequence of sin and spiritual death. Through Adam's sin, the door of destruction opened wide to many formidable foes, including physical death and disease. **Sin effectively preempted God's original plan**, revolutionizing the glory and grandeur of his creation.

Then, because of his treachery, God judged Satan, declaring his ultimate defeat by "one who would bruise his head."[8] This prophetic utterance promised a Savior who would purchase our deliverance from Satan's kingdom of death and destruction.

Through His death on the cross, Jesus, the only begotten Son of God, would defeat Satan and bring freedom from the burden of sin and spiritual death.

---

[7] Ge 5:4-5
[8] Ge 3:15

Yet the world as we know it today continues to suffer from sin's corruption. According to the apostle Paul, it longs for the day it will "join God's children in glorious freedom from death and decay."[9] In spite of the beauty we see in snow-capped mountains, rolling seas, and lush green valleys, the earth is held in bondage and therefore cannot measure up to the artistry of the Garden of Eden. But one day, Jesus will come for His church, and then, man AND creation will be set free from all the effects of sin.[10] On that day, sin and every encumbrance of sin will finally surrender to the hand of God.

Oh, what a glorious day!

DEATH AND DISEASE

After God's word to Satan, He introduced man's enemy, physical death. He spoke to Adam, saying:

Dust thou art, and unto dust shalt thou return.[11]

This describes physical death! **Physical death was birthed by sin and spiritual death.** Because Adam and

---

9 Rm 8:21, NLT, Biblegateway.com
10 Rm 8:19-21
11 Ge 3:19

Eve ate of the tree of the knowledge of good and evil, spiritual death dominated them, and they became children of Satan. Their separation from God and subsequent union with Satan was the catalyst of physical death and the introduction of disease.

Just as a rock thrown in a pond forms concentric circles which move toward the shore, spiritual death sent ripples of destruction into the physical body where death's closest allies, pain and disease, stood ready to hold man hostage.

> *The trauma of disease caused by sin and death is a curse.*

The word *disease* itself confirms this. The prefix "dis" means separation and the word "ease" is defined as the state of being comfortable.[12] Therefore, dis-ease is separation from ease or comfort. This graphically explains our struggle with pain and sickness. Both are rooted in sin, promoted by spiritual death, and if unaided by natural recovery and healing power, will introduce our enemy physical death.

Yet, **through Christ, our struggle with sin, spiritual death, and disease is ended**. Satan's kingdom, the kingdom of destruction, has been conquered, and the tyranny of sin that separated us from God is broken.[13]

---

[12] Webster's 1959
[13] Col 1:13-14

The anguish of disease birthed by sin and spiritual death has been defeated by the risen Lord.

Healing power now carries us to victory. Our great and mighty God is the Lord, our Physician! The sacrifice of Jesus has set us free and healing is ours!

CHAPTER 3

ONE REMEDY FOR TWO THINGS

We have the witness of the Scripture that Adam's sin brought spiritual death, or separation from God, to man. Spiritual death opened the door to physical death, and physical death gave place to disease.

> *But God has provided a solution, one remedy, for both sin and sickness.*

God's remedy for man's plight from the Old Testament to the New is the shedding of blood, first of an animal and then the precious blood of His Son, Jesus.

The Word of God records that without the shedding of blood, there is no remission of sin.[1] It further testifies by the wounds of Jesus we have been healed.[2] These Scriptural declarations confirm **Jesus' blood paid the price for man's freedom.**

> *His sacrifice was the only remedy for sin and sickness.*

PASSOVER

This valuable truth of "one remedy for two things"

---

[1] Heb 9:22
[2] 1Pe 2:24

is easily seen in the record of Israel's deliverance from Egyptian bondage. For several centuries, Israel was oppressed by Pharaoh, held in bondage as brick makers and laborers who built Pharaoh's fortified cities. At God's command, Moses went to Pharaoh and said, "Let my people go, that they may hold a feast unto me in the wilderness."[3] Pharaoh, however, denied this request, commanding that more work be given to God's people. He also refused to send them the supplies to make the bricks, yet they had to keep producing the same quota. When they could not meet his requirement, they were beaten.[4]

Pharaoh could not be dissuaded from his harsh stand against God's people, though great judgments fell upon the land. Not until the death of Egypt's firstborn children and animals, did he relent. He called for Moses saying, "Go, serve the Lord, as ye have said."[5]

It is interesting to note that there were more than two million men, plus women and children, in the Israelite camp.[6] Yet, when Pharaoh let them leave Egypt, the Psalmist records, "There was not one feeble person among their tribes."[7] The word "feeble" means to waver through weakness of the legs, to stumble, faint or fall.[8] It

---

[3] Ex 5:1
[4] Ex 5:8,14
[5] Ex 12:31
[6] Ex 12:37, *Barnes, Clark*
[7] Ps 105:37
[8] H3782, Strong's

is beyond reason that not one feeble person could be found – not even a workman who had been beaten.

No one was suffering. What an amazing report!

On the night Israel was delivered from their bondage in Egypt, they celebrated the Lord's Passover. God instructed them to slay a lamb and put the blood of the lamb on the doorposts and the lintel of the house.[9] He said the destroyer was coming through Egypt that night to kill every firstborn child and beast, but everyone that remained behind the blood placed on the doorposts and lintel would be protected. The blood would save them from the judgment to fall on Egypt.

The Israelites were further instructed to roast the flesh of the lamb and eat it with unleavened bread and bitter herbs. They must eat it with their shoes on and their staff in their hand. God declared:

Eat it in haste: it is the Lord's passover.[10]

The Passover lamb sacrificed by Israel was a type, or pattern, of the sacrifice of Jesus. A pattern is a likeness, a guide, a model or a representative form. When you sew clothes for your family, you use a

---

[9] Ex 12:7
[10] Ex 12:11

pattern. The pattern represents the item you are making and enables you to sew it together properly. It is a picture of the finished product. The sacrificed animal represented the work of Christ and envisioned His death on the cross. It was the provision of God until the death of Jesus, our Lord.

Through the blood of the animal, Israel was protected from death. By eating the lamb, they were strengthened for their journey. The Passover lamb quickened their bodies so that not one feeble person remained among them.

> *The blood sacrifice and the Passover meal were God's remedy for sin and sickness.*

Was there then one remedy for two things? Yes, decidedly yes! The Passover celebration declares it!

LEVITICUS

In the early chapters of Leviticus, God instructed Moses to offer animal sacrifices for sin. Many different sins are mentioned, but each of them decreed the death of an unblemished animal. The death of the animal made atonement for sin.

The Old Testament word *atonement* means to

cover.[11] When you put your hand in a glove, it is covered by the fabric of the glove. In like manner, **the sacrifice of the animal only covered sin.** It did not remit, blot out, or erase sin.

The writer of Hebrews declares:

It is not possible that the blood of bulls and of goats should take away sins.[12]

But, oh, what glorious news! **Jesus put away or cancelled sin by the sacrifice of Himself.**

Yet, through God's Old Testament provision of atonement, sins such as deception, theft, and extortion were covered and forgiven. Ceremonial uncleanness, broken vows, and acts of disobedience were also covered. Each sin, whether intentionally or ignorantly committed, was atoned by an animal sacrifice. This sacrifice was the only remedy for sin until Jesus' death on the cross. His death provided remittance for the sins of man. They were pardoned as if they had never been committed.

Now, it is important to note that in these early chapters of Leviticus, there is no mention of an atoning sacrifice for disease. However, if we continue reading

---

[11] H3722, Strong's
[12] Heb 10:4

God's holy commands, in Leviticus 14, we are face to face with this powerful truth. Here, the Scripture talks about leprosy, which is, of course, a disease.[13] It is not a sin like those previously listed. Yet the law of cleansing for the leper is very similar to the law of atonement for sin.

For many, it is beyond imagination that there was a blood sacrifice for disease. But the Word of God is definite. Through the sacrifice of animals, atonement was made for the leper. The priest offered a sin offering, a trespass offering, and a burnt offering, and the leper was cleansed.

Now, I think this is most interesting – **a sin offering and a trespass offering were offered for a disease.** Could this be because sickness, like physical death, was born of Satan through Adam's sin? Yes!

> *Spiritual death, physical death and disease have one foundation, and therefore, one remedy.*

JESUS

The Passover celebration and the sacrifices of Leviticus are patterns of the accomplishments of Jesus' death and resurrection. Through the Passover celebration and these Old Testament sacrifices, God

---

[13] Lev 14:2

provided forgiveness and healing for His people just as in the New Testament, **Jesus' blood bought our freedom and victory over sin and sickness.**

Jesus is God's eternal provision for the need of man.

The apostle Peter confirms this with his words in 1 Peter 2:24. He states:

Who his own self bare our sins in his own body on the tree, that we, being dead to sins, should live unto righteousness: by whose stripes ye were healed.

The tree mentioned in this verse is the cross on which Jesus died. When Jesus shed His blood in death, He carried our sins, blotting them out so that we could live in righteousness. But did you notice He also suffered for our healing?

Some have said that the healing mentioned here is "spiritual healing," or healing for the spirit of man. Yet the Bible declares, when a man is born again, his spirit is NEW, not healed or restored. The apostle Paul reports:

> *Therefore if any man be in Christ, he is a new creature.*[14]

The Phillips translation of this same verse says, "If a man is in Christ he becomes a new person altogether." Therefore, the phrase "spiritual healing" could not apply to Jesus' work for man's spirit, but the healing mentioned here must reference the physical body. Unlike the spirit of man, the physical body can be healed or restored; it is never new.

The fullness, the grandeur, of God's sacrifice for our body and our spirit is also presented in the ordinance of Holy Communion. In this celebration given to the church, there are two elements – the bread, which represents Jesus' body broken for our healing, and the wine that portrays His blood shed for our sin. Together, these elements proclaim His death.

The Scripture says:

> *For as often as you eat this bread and drink this cup, you proclaim the Lord's death till he come.*[15]

---

[14] 2Co 5:17
[15] 1Co 11:26 NKJV

By partaking of the bread and the cup, we declare the totality of God's sacrifice for sin and sickness.

So, is there one remedy for these two things, sin and sickness? Yes! The Passover Celebration declares it, and the animal sacrifices of Leviticus portray it. The cross establishes it, and every time we partake of Holy Communion, we remember it. The blood of our Lord Jesus Christ has blotted out our sins and healed our diseases. The Word of God has spoken!

CHAPTER 4

THE SHADOW OF THE CROSS

God's great plan of redemption through Jesus' death on the cross was declared by many Old Testament events. One outstanding Old Testament event that paints a picture of Jesus' death for sin and sickness is found in Numbers 16:41. Here, an angry Israel did what a lot of people do – they complained about leadership. Now, let me point out, murmuring against leadership is a mistake. It is really a mistake. In fact, when we study the Scripture carefully, we learn that God forbids complaining.[1]

As a result of Israel's grumbling and complaining about their leaders, a plague began among the people and over fourteen thousand people died. Yet God was willing to forgive Israel and heal them. When Moses ordered Aaron to put on incense and make atonement for the people, the plague ceased.

> *This event in the life of Israel definitely points us toward the cross. Through the atonement, the chilling effect of sin, sickness, and death was eliminated in God's people, and the shadow of the cross was cast in our hearts.*

---

[1] Php 2:14

THE BRASS SERPENT

The work of the cross is exemplified again in Numbers 21. Once more, the people of Israel spoke against leadership. This time, however, they also questioned God, allowing discouragement to dispute His provision of food and water. As a result, serpents invaded the camp and many people died. It is interesting to note that serpents and scorpions had always been in the wilderness,[2] but it was not until the onslaught of sin that the lives of the people were endangered.

A repentant Israel soon came to Moses and confessed their sin. They petitioned him to pray, asking God to take away the serpents, and as Moses prayed, the Lord instructed him to make a serpent of brass and set it on a pole. God declared:

"Make a fiery serpent, and set it on a pole; and it shall be that everyone who is bitten, when he looks at it, shall live."[3]

In this passage, the word "looks" is very important. Obviously, you cannot look at the serpent on the pole and at the same time watch the serpents on the ground.

---

[2] Deu 8:15
[3] Num 21:8 NKJV

You must either lift your eyes upward to the pole or cast them downward toward your feet.

When children watch a television program or a sports enthusiast follows the big game, they are intensely observing the drama in front of them. If you need them, it doesn't matter how loud you call, they simply cannot be distracted. In this same manner, God's people, Israel, must not be distracted. In order to be healed, they must focus on the brass serpent.

Jesus referenced this Old Testament event when He proclaimed the work of the cross to Nicodemus. He told him, "You must be born again," and compared the brass serpent on the pole to the Son of God on the cross.[4] This comparison confirms God's completed work for sin and sickness, proving that our sins are remitted and our bodies are healed when our heart turns to our risen Lord.

The trite religious notion that healing was not provided through Jesus' death is therefore without foundation.

> *If the Savior's suffering did not free men of sin AND disease, we surely cannot believe that Israel was forgiven and then healed by looking at a serpent on a pole.*

---

[4] Jn 3:7 NLT

THE SHADOW

We cannot sever these Old Testament examples from New Testament reality because the book of Hebrews declares:

> *The old system in the law of Moses was only a shadow of the things to come, not the reality of the good things Christ has done for us.*[5]

In the New Century Version, we read:

> *The law is only an unclear picture of the good things coming in the future.*

A shadow is an obscure image of some person, place, or thing that is created by light.[6] As an obscure picture, or a shadow, **the law was a visual representation of Christ and the good things He would do as our Redeemer.**

What the shadow of the law envisioned, the New

---

[5] Heb 10:1 NLT
[6] MW

Testament has fully declared. The Old Testament image of Jesus cast by the prophet Isaiah – "unto us a son is given" – was unveiled in Jesus, the only begotten Son of God, born of a virgin.[7]

Isaiah's vision of One brought as a lamb to the slaughter[8] was uncovered in the New Testament record of the apostle Peter:

> *Who his own self bare our sins in his own body on the tree. [9]*

The words of the psalmist, "Thou wilt not leave my soul in hell"[10] come to light when God raised Jesus up, "having loosed the pains of death."[11]

Many Old Testament scholars communicated the work of God later completed in the New Covenant.

> *There is no doubt that a picture of the cross was revealed by those who walked with God long before Jesus was born of a virgin in Bethlehem.*

---

[7] Is 7:14; Is 9:6
[8] Is 53:7
[9] 1Pe 2:24
[10] Ps 16:10
[11] Act 2:24

Through their words, **the image of the cross is drawn for us.** In the Old Testament, the psalmist gave testimony to the rage and tumult that brought Jesus before the Sanhedrin and Pontius Pilate, where His crucifixion was decreed.[12] The price of Judas Iscariot's betrayal of Jesus – thirty pieces of silver – is recorded by the prophet, Zechariah.[13] He then brings us to the foot of the cross with his words:

They shall look upon me [Jesus] whom they have pierced."[14]

The agony of Jesus' crucifixion was captured by the psalmist when he declared:

In my thirst they gave me [Jesus] vinegar to drink."[15]

But the psalmist didn't stop there. He also proclaimed Jesus' Resurrection and ascension when he

---

[12] Ps 2:1-2; Lk 23:21-24
[13] Zec 11:12
[14] Zec 12:10
[15] Ps 69:21

said:

The Lord said unto my Lord, Sit thou at my right hand, until I make thine enemies thy footstool.[16]

These verses paint the image of the cross in our inward man and enable us to gratefully embrace Jesus' sacrifice with all its benefits. Benefits that Psalm 103 counsels us to remember. We are not surprised that forgiveness AND healing are listed among these benefits because **from Genesis to Revelation the Word of God confirms that Jesus' death remitted our sins AND healed our bodies of disease.**

Today, the benefits revealed by the Old Testament writers are available through our faith in the finished work of the Lord Jesus Christ. The law, which proclaimed His sacrificial death for sin and sickness, has been fulfilled and every blessing is ours through Jesus, our risen Lord. The shadow of the law has become reality in the face of our risen Lord and healing is ours! Oh, what glorious news!

---

[16] Ps 110:1

CHAPTER 5

WE HAVE LIFT OFF

In Isaiah 53, centuries before Jesus' death on the cross, the prophet Isaiah painted a precise picture of God's great plan of redemption. By the Spirit, he envisioned the final days of our Lord's life on earth and the purpose of His sacrifice. What a blessing this prophetic utterance is to us! It overwhelmingly proves that Jesus' death was the payment for sin AND sickness and disease.

Now, there is no question in the minds of God's people that Jesus died as the payment for sin. As we read Isaiah 53, we note that:

He was wounded for our transgressions, he was bruised for our iniquities.[1]

We believe this truth! Yet many times, we don't believe Jesus' death paid to heal our diseases. The prophet Isaiah's response to our doubt is found in verse four of this chapter.

The King James Version reads:

---

[1] Is 53:5

Surely he [Jesus] hath borne our griefs, and carried our sorrows.

The Amplified Version says:

Surely He [Jesus] has borne our griefs (sickness, weakness, and distress) and carried our sorrows and pains [of punishment].

Then the Jewish Publication Society Bible writes:

Surely our diseases he did bear, and our pains he carried.

These scholarly works confirm that Jesus also died for our sicknesses by translating the word **griefs** as **sickness and disease**, and the word **sorrows** as **pain**.[2]

These same words, here translated "griefs" and "sorrows", are observed in other Scriptures, further establishing their relationship to disease and pain. For

---

[2] H2483, H4341, Strong's

example, in 2 Chronicles 16:12, the word translated *griefs*, the Hebrew word *choliy*, is used to describe King Asa who "was diseased [choliy] in his feet."

It is also written in 2 Kings 1:2 where King Ahaziah fell through a lattice and did not recover from the "disease", which is again the Hebrew word *choliy*, that resulted from that accident. Another example is recorded in in 1 Kings 17:17 when a child "fell sick; and his sickness [choliy] was so sore, that there was no breath left in him." In these Scriptures, both words, "sickness" and "disease", are translated from the Hebrew word *choliy*, the same word translated "griefs" in Isaiah 53.

A study of the word *sorrows* in Isaiah 53 again proves that the sacrifice of Jesus was for disease as well as sin. Here, the word **"sorrows"** comes from the Hebrew word "makob", and it **means anguish, affliction, and pain.** This anguish and pain is ably described in Job 33:19-22 where Elihu speaks of an emaciated man overwhelmed with pain and very close to death. This is an obvious reference to the pain and trauma of disease.

With this understanding, we embrace a very important truth. **The sacrifice of Jesus included freedom from the burden of sickness and pain.** When Jesus bore our sins through His death on the cross, there is no doubt He bore our diseases at the same time.

JESUS BORE AND CARRIED

The prophet Isaiah recorded:

> *[Jesus] hath BORNE our griefs, and CARRIED our sorrows."*[3]

From our study, we are certain this verse declares **Jesus bore and carried our diseases and pains**. This magnificent truth is further enhanced when we define the two verbs *borne* and *carried*.

Our first verb, **borne**, is translated from the Hebrew word "nasa", **meaning to lift**. It conveys the idea of lifting a burden in order to carry it away.[4] It is very interesting that this word is the acronym for the National Aeronautics and Space Administration. Many times, from our home in Florida, we have seen the rockets launched by NASA. As the rocket leaves the launching pad and travels into the atmosphere, a commentator ordinarily says, "We have lift off!" This is the precise meaning of this Hebrew word.

> *Jesus has lifted the burden of our sicknesses and carried them away.* **Through Him, "We have lift off."**

The work of our sanitation and refuse services is

---

[3] Is 53:4, author's emphasis
[4] McCrossan, pg. 13

another illustration clarifying the meaning of the phrase "lift off." Although we live over 100 yards from a paved road, every Monday we faithfully carry our garbage cans down the driveway and leave them for pickup. Our sanitation personnel remove our refuse by lifting our garbage cans and emptying them into their truck. Through their services, "We have lift off."

Now, according to biblical scholars, our next verb, **"carried"**, is derived from the Hebrew word "sabal" and **emphasizes the weight of the burden** being carried.[5] When we declare the Jesus bore our griefs and carried our sorrows, **we understand that a HEAVY load was lifted off and taken away**.

The Knox translation projects this truth saying:

Our weakness, and it was he who carried the weight of it, our miseries, and it was he who bore them."[6]

I love this translation because it describes griefs and sorrows as weakness and misery and then it states HE CARRIED THE WEIGHT of them. HE BORE them.

There are not too many events in life

---

[5] McCrossan, Pg. 13
[6] Is 53:4 Knox

*that bring greater misery than sickness
and disease.*

It doesn't matter if it is a headache or something more devastating. If we are sick, we are miserable and we want to be released from this burden. But here's the good news we have learned—**Jesus carried the heavy burden of sickness.** Oh, what a wonderful Savior!

THE PRICE

Sickness and pain are tools of Satan designed to bind, restrict, overpower, and tyrannize us. But when Jesus died and after three days rose again, **Satan was defeated and the destructive power of sickness and pain was conquered.** For this reason, when sickness attacks us and pain unsettles us, we can stand secure in the work of Christ.

*He was the ransom for our sins AND
diseases.*

The word "ransom" is familiar to us as the price paid to release someone from captivity. In exchange for a certain amount of money, a kidnapped person will be set free, or rescued. Of course, there is no sum or money or any good deed that can free us from the bondage of sin or disease.

The Scripture confirms this in 1 Peter 1:18 when it

declares we were not "redeemed with corruptible things, as silver and gold." Also, in Titus 3:5, the apostle Paul writes that our salvation was "not by works of righteousness which we have done." Instead, we were redeemed by the precious blood of our Lord Jesus Christ.[7]

Through Jesus' blood, we are ransomed from the onslaught of disease and pain. Our release from these foes is magnificently described by Elihu in Job 33:24-25. He said:

> "I have found a ransom. His flesh shall be fresher than a child's: he shall return to the days of his youth."

Here, his words obviously describe freedom from sickness. Because a ransom was paid, the captive was released from the bondage of disease and pain and returned to health.

Jesus' sacrifice was the ransom for ALL our sin and for EVERY disease. According to the Scripture, He was:

> ...preaching the Good News of the

---

[7] 1Pe 1:19

Kingdom, and healing every disease and every sickness among the people.[8]

Today, He still heals every sickness and every disease. He is "Jesus Christ the same yesterday, and to day, and for ever."[9] Oh, what great love! What a wonderful Savior! What a sacrifice!

---

[8] Mt 4:23 WEB
[9] Heb 13:8

CHAPTER 6

THE CROSS AND THE BLOOD

The magnificence of man's rescue through Jesus' sacrificial death pictured in the Old Testament comes to full light in the New Testament record. Here, we walk with Jesus to the cross, gaze in the empty tomb, and witness His resurrection. After His ascension into heaven, we sit expectantly with the disciples and all those assembled awaiting the Day of Pentecost. What a blessing!

The gospels tell the story of these blessed events, but it is the epistles that enlarge our understanding. Through the apostle Paul and others, we see clearly the grandeur of God's plan and comprehend the depths of Jesus' death and resurrection.

> *We learn that we were baptized with Jesus in death, raised with Him to eternal life, and seated with Him in heavenly places. He has given us victory!*

Our great victory through Jesus' death and resurrection begins when we acknowledge man's sin.

In Isaiah 53:6, we read:

> *All we like sheep have gone astray; we have turned every one to his own way; and the Lord hath LAID on him the iniquity of us all.*[1]

The apostle Paul simply says, "For all have sinned, and come short of the glory of God."[2]

This is not a startling fact to us. We recognize man's sinful nature. But what wonderful news is ours! Through the sacrifice of Jesus Christ, we have been rescued. When we trust Jesus as our Savior and Lord, we are given eternal life.

Isaiah 53:6 notes that man's sin was LAID on Jesus. The apostle Peter explained this when he wrote:

> *Who his own self bear our sins in his OWN body on the tree.*[3]

The tree mentioned here is the cross where Jesus died as our substitute. He paid man's debt — a debt that we owed but could not pay.

---

[1] Author's emphasis
[2] Rm 3:23
[3] 1Pe 2:24, author's emphasis

In 2 Corinthians 5:21, we read:

For God made Christ, who never sinned, to be the offering for our sin, so that we could be made right with God through Christ."[4]

These verses conclusively prove that **Jesus died as man's substitute.**

A number of years ago, I read in the newspaper about a lady who did not pay her parking tickets. She'd let them accumulate, ignoring any notices for payment until eventually she had to go to court. The court subsequently sentenced her to a number of days in jail. However, her husband petitioned the court, asking if he could go in her place, and the judge granted his request. This dear husband stepped forward as her substitute and took the punishment she deserved. She didn't go to jail because he went for her.

Jesus, in the same manner, took on man's punishment. If man had been left to pay for his own sin, he would be in hell unable to escape because he was being justly punished. Jesus, on the other hand, was the sinless Son of God. **He didn't go to hell as a sinner, but as the substitute for man.** He was our mediator, reconciling us to God.

---

[4] NLT

> *According to Vine's Complete Expository Dictionary, the word "reconciliation" indicates "change, from enmity to friendship."[5]*

This reconciliation to God was accomplished when our sin was LAID on Jesus, and then after three days and nights in the place of damnation, He defeated Satan and was raised in victory with the keys of death and hell.[6] **Jesus' victory over the principalities and powers of hell was FOR US.** Through Him, we are delivered from Satan's power and translated into God's kingdom.[7]

THE BLOOD OF JESUS

Jesus' sacrifice wasn't for ONE man or even for a FEW men, but for the entire world. Isaiah 53:5 declares:

> *But he was wounded for OUR transgressions, he was bruised for OUR iniquities: the chastisement of OUR peace was upon him; and with his stripes WE are healed.[8]*

---

[5] Vines1
[6] Rev 1:18
[7] Col 1:13
[8] Author's emphasis

This "our," this "we," as defined in John 3:16, is the world. In the well-known verse, Jesus said, "For God so loved the world, that he gave His only begotten son." This means that anyone who will receive Jesus' sacrifice and declare Him as their Lord will be saved.

Through Jesus' death, the price was paid for sin and every consequence of sin. **The price, of course, was not money, but the sacrifice of Jesus' life—His own shed blood.**

In 1 Peter 1:18-19 we read:

> *Forasmuch as ye know that ye were not redeemed with corruptible things, as silver and gold, from your vain conversation received by tradition from your fathers; but with the precious blood of Christ.*

This verse decrees that we "were not redeemed with corruptible things," but we were redeemed with something more 'precious."

I love the word "precious." We speak of babies as precious, or dear and beloved. We say, "Oh, how precious." Water in the desert is also precious. I know if I were in the desert and someone brought me a canteen filled with water, it would be precious. Water has great value because it preserves life. The artwork of the great masters is also precious. Their work is irreplaceable, and therefore, of high price.

> *In these same ways, Jesus' blood is precious. It is dear and beloved, greatly valued and highly esteemed. Nothing can replace it. No other blood sets men free. No other blood gives life. Jesus' blood is the only answer for sinful man.*

FREEDOM FROM SIN AND SICKNESS

It is through the blood of Jesus that man's sins are remitted, or blotted out, AND his diseases are healed. We learned this magnificent truth when we studied Isaiah 53. In this chapter, the prophet Isaiah declared that Jesus bore (*nasa*) and carried (*sabal*) our sins AND our sickness.

When the apostle Matthew explained the healing ministry of Jesus, he referenced this inspired word from Isaiah.

In Matthew 8:16-17, we read:

> *[Jesus] healed all that were sick: That it might be fulfilled which was spoken by Esaias the prophet, saying, Himself took our infirmities, and bare our sicknesses.*

In this passage, I particularly like the word HIMSELF. Jesus sacrificed HIMSELF. The writer of Hebrews voiced this truth when he said:

He [Jesus] had by HIMSELF purged our sins.[9]

The apostle Peter agreed declaring, "Who HIS OWN SELF bare our sins."[10]

Then he writes:

By whose stripes [we] were healed.[11]

Through these verses, we are assured that the sacrifice of Jesus for sin also included freedom from disease.

JESUS, OUR HEALER

Jesus freed man from both sin and sickness. We dare not eliminate either from the plan and purpose of God. **We cannot embrace freedom from sin and deny**

---

[9] Heb 1:3, author's emphasis
[10] Author's emphasis
[11] 1Pe 2:24

the price He paid for sickness and disease. Certainly, the testimony of Isaiah, Peter, and Paul prove this beyond a shadow of a doubt.

Yet some have attempted to undermine this powerful truth by teaching that healing is for the spirit, not for the physical body. However, when a man is born again, his spirit is made new. It is not healed. Healing is a restoration of the tissues to soundness.[12] When a body is healed, the damaged and diseased tissue is repaired or replaced, but other parts of the body function as usual. In the same way, if you restore or refurbish an older piece of furniture, it is both new and old. It may be covered with new fabric and it may contain a new support system, but it is not completely new.

Through Jesus Christ's death, our spirit is new. It is not healed or restored. It is not partially new or almost new. **It is completely new.** The apostle Paul validates this saying:

Therefore if any man be in Christ, he is a new creature: old things are passed away; behold, all things are become new.[13]

---

[12] Webster's
[13] 2Co 5:17

The testimony of the New Living Translation explains this truth.

What this means is that those who become Christians become new persons.

The Message Bible declares:

Anyone united with the Messiah gets a fresh start, is created new.

When I received Jesus as my Savior and Lord, I did not realize that I was given a new spirit. In fact, I didn't know I was a spirit being. However, I did know that my body and mind were not new. I looked the same and, because my mind was not renewed, I acted the same. Yet I *was* new, and over time I was changed by the work of God that began that day in my NEW spirit.

As I grew in God, I learned many valuable truths, but how marvelous it was when I found out that Jesus was my Healer. I was studying the Scripture one day in order to substitute for a new friend who was teaching a Bible study group. The lesson was on divine healing, and I was very intimidated because I didn't know anything about healing. I really had never given it any thought. But that week, as I poured over the Word of God, verse after verse spoke clearly to me, and I recognized Jesus was our Healer.

This was the beginning of many years of study. Today, I am fully surrendered to Jesus as my Healer. Boldly, I say, "[God] sent His Word, and healed [me]."[14] Certainly, this is the truth. I have no doubt!

---

[14] Ps 107:20

CHAPTER 7

I'VE BEEN REDEEMED!

Every Christmas, my heart returns to the prophecy of Zacharias given after the birth of John the Baptist. This Word from the Lord always prepares me for the birth of our Savior because it highlights the purpose of His coming. It begins:

> *Blessed be the Lord God of Israel; for he hath visited and redeemed his people.*[1]

Then it declares Jesus came as the horn, or strength, of salvation to save us from our enemies.[2] This was the purpose of His visit. **He came to redeem man from his enemy.** But what is "redemption"?

> *The word "redeem" means to ransom or to purchase back something that has been lost.*[3]

---

[1] Lk 1:68
[2] Lk 1:69,71,74
[3] G3085, Strong's;*Easton*

In our community, if your pet is found roaming the street, the local officials will capture him and take him to their kennel. Then if he's tagged properly, they'll call you. However, if you go to pick him up, they're not going to give him to you once you arrive. He's no longer under your authority, but under theirs, and there's a fee for their services. You will have to pay the price to buy him back.

> *This is the first key to redemption. It always requires the payment of a price.*

If you inherit your grandmother's ring and subsequently decide you don't want it, you can take it to a pawn shop, and there, they may buy the ring from you. But if you later regret your decision, wondering, "Why did I do that?" Just like the county animal services, the pawn shop is not going to give the ring back to you. You must redeem it, or buy it back.

In the life of my own grandmother, following my grandfather's passing, she could no longer live on her own, so the family moved her to a senior citizen high-rise in town. Of course, they had to sell some of her furniture because it wouldn't all fit in the smaller space. In the process of downsizing, a French buffet, or sideboard, she was particularly attached to was sold. The family was not aware of how important that sideboard was to her. But she was heartbroken and talked about it all the time, until eventually, the family members became desperate to find it. They wanted to buy it back, even if it required double the price.

> *This is the second key of redemption. Redemption comes with a strong desire for that which was lost. Love, affection, or longing prompt you to pay whatever price is required.*

This heartfelt struggle causes you to buy back the ring, to repurchase your dog, or in my grandmother's case, to locate the sideboard.

> *In other words, redemption includes motivation.*

When someone brings my husband a piece of furniture to restore, it usually comes to him in very poor condition, broken and worn. One particular piece he received was brought to him in a garbage bag. The family wanted it reassembled. Now, to outsiders, this piece of furniture didn't look like much, but to them it held value. They desired to see it whole and sound again, and though repairs would cost more than it was worth, they were willing to pay the price.

GOD'S PART

In like manner, God's strong desire – His great love – sent Jesus as the sacrifice for man's sin. **Jesus came to redeem man because of God's great mercy.** He came to pay the price for man's freedom. He did not come to condemn man or to point His finger at exposed sin. Instead, **He came to blot out man's transgressions.**

The prophet Isaiah said Jesus blotted out sin "for his own sake."[4] Every parent who truly loves their children understands the desire to bless or rescue a child, not exclusively for the child's sake, but "for their own sake." On holidays and birthdays, we plan extravagant events and stretch our budget because our heart demands it. Though a new computer or two-hundred dollar tennis shoes are far beyond our capability, we find a way to purchase them because we love our children.

> Jesus came because "God so loved the world."[5] He came to bring light to those in the darkness of sin and spiritual death. Jesus' sacrifice rescued man and ended the rule of Satan.

THE WELL THOUGHT-OUT PLAN OF GOD

From the foundation of the world, God purposed to

---

[4] Is 43:25, author's paraphrase
[5] Jn 3:16

redeem man. When man sinned, He was not taken by surprise, saying, "What are we going to do? Look at man; look what he's done." No, **God gave man a choice, and He knew man would make the wrong choice.** Adam and Eve were commanded not to eat from the tree of the knowledge of good and evil, but they yielded to Satan's wiles and, through their disobedience, sin reigned.

Long before the sin of Adam and Eve, God had determined to rescue man from disobedience and death.

On the day of Pentecost, the apostle Peter explained this preordained plan. He said that Jesus was delivered to death by "the determinate counsel and foreknowledge of God."[6] The phrase *the determinate counsel and foreknowledge of God* is translated by The Message Bible, "the deliberate and well-thought-out plan of God." The New Living Bible says the, "prearranged plan" of God.[7] Both of these translations highlight God's predetermined plan of rescue.

Often, when we take our daughter and granddaughter to lunch, no one has a plan. One person says, "How about barbeque?" The other suggests the sandwich shop. We can't decide.

---

[6] Act 2:22-24
[7] NLT, Biblegateway.com

But God wasn't caught without a plan.
He sent Jesus, and Jesus fulfilled God's
plan and accomplished His purpose.

He was God's lamb without spot or blemish, and in the mind of God, He was slain before the foundation of the world. In 1 Peter 1:20 we read:

[Jesus] was foreordained before the foundation of the world, but was manifest in these last times for you.

This was God's predetermined plan, a plan so secure that He considered it done even before Jesus was born in human flesh.

REDEEMED FROM SICKNESS

Through God's magnificent plan of redemption, Satan's onslaught was ended. According to Colossians 2:15, when Jesus died on the cross He triumphed over Satan. In the King James Bible, we read that the principalities and powers of Satan were "spoiled."

The New Living Translations says:

> God disarmed the evil rulers and
> authorities.

In the New Century Version, we read, "God stripped the spiritual rulers and powers of their authority." Through the cross, Jesus openly, publicly, declared Satan's defeat.

> When Satan was defeated, we were
> redeemed from sin and every
> consequence of sin. This includes
> sickness and disease.

Without question, sickness is a work of Satan. He is the thief who comes to kill, steal, and destroy.[8] Certainly, sickness kills! Sickness destroys! Sickness steals!

Sickness is also a curse! In Deuteronomy 28, this is plainly stated. Here, many different diseases are mentioned including mental and emotional disorders, but each of them is a curse. In fact, according to Deuteronomy 28: 61, every sickness and every disease is a curse.

Yet in Galatians 3:13, the apostle Paul writes:

---

[8] Jn 10:10

*Christ hath redeemed us from the
curse of the law, being made a curse
for us: for it is written, Cursed is every
one that hangeth on a tree.*

In this verse, notice the use of the past tense verb *redeemed*. "Christ hath redeemed us." He is not going to redeem us in the future; He will not return to the cross again to redeem us. No, when He hung on the cross, He paid the price for every sin and every disease and through our faith in Him, we are redeemed. We are free!

I AM REDEEMED

The bold declaration of every Christian is, "I am God's child. I am in His kingdom. He is my Father, and through the sacrifice of His only begotten Son, Jesus, I have been set free. I am free from the curse of sin and sickness. I am redeemed." **This confession does not mean that sin and sickness do not exist.** Both are in our world. Sin exists! Sickness exists! However, **they have been defeated by our risen Lord.**

Oh, how helpful that realization is to my heart! Sin and sickness have been defeated. They have been defeated because Satan was defeated. However, he has not been eliminated from the earth. He still roams our land seeking to destroy us.[9] He still chooses to kill.

*But God always desires to heal us. God
promotes prosperity and health.*

Satan cannot conquer my faith in God or destroy my
trust in God's magnificent redemptive plan. I know that
through the sacrifice of the Lord Jesus Christ my sins are
remitted and my body is healed. In Christ, I am whole. I
am sound. I am well. This is God's great redemptive
plan, and I believe in His plan! Certainly, I've been
redeemed!

---

[9] 1Pe 5:8

SECTION 2

NO MORE CONFUSION

Howbeit when he, the Spirit of truth, is come, he will guide you into all truth (Jn 16:13).

CHAPTER 8

PAUL'S THORN – DEVIL OR DISEASE?

In Paul's letter to the saints at Philippi, he discussed an important decision – to live and help the churches under his care or to die and be with His Lord. As he pondered this decision, He wrote:

For I am in a strait betwixt two, having a desire to depart, and to be with Christ; which is far better: Nevertheless to abide in the flesh is more needful for you.[1]

Everyone knows how difficult it can be to make a choice, especially when you are deciding between two great entrées at your favorite restaurant. Suddenly, you are torn between two or more desires.[2] Then, after you order and your food is delivered, you find yourself wondering if the other entrée would have been a better choice. This explains Paul's dilemma. He knew to die was gain, but he was also sure the churches needed him.[3] Finally, he chose to live and continue feeding them with

---

[1] Php 1:23-24
[2] Php 1:23 NLT, author's paraphrase
[3] Php 1:21,24

the knowledge and revelation God had given him.

In 2 Corinthians 12, we learn why this was such a hard choice for Paul. Here, he tells us that he had been in the third heaven, the realm of God's glory. He said, "I knew a man in Christ ... caught up to the third heaven."[4] Although Paul writes this in the third person, scholars tell us he was talking about himself. This was a common form of address in that day.[5]

What a phenomenal trip this must have been! Paul was in the third heaven, the home of God, and it is interesting to note that he didn't know if he was still clothed with his physical body. In effect, he said, "I'm not even going to try to figure this out. God knows if I was in body or only in spirit. I don't."[6] Amazing!

Now, we better understand Paul's statement. After this overwhelming experience, the choice to stay on earth or go to heaven was difficult indeed. My, the draw of heaven and glory!

BOASTING

Paul's experience in the glorious home of our God promoted him in God's earthly kingdom. It was not necessary, as some report, for Paul to boast constantly of himself. After all, if you had been in heaven and received visions and revelations from the Lord, you

---

[4] 2Co 12:2
[5] 2Co 12:2, Barnes
[6] 2Co 12:2, author's paraphrase

would not need to promote yourself. People would that for you. Further, if you, at that time, understood the purpose of the cross, Jesus' descent into hell, and Satan's subsequent defeat, your knowledge would exalt you. There is no doubt that Paul's revelation of the mysteries of God and his heavenly vision exalted him.

The Scripture warns us about the dangers of boasting and exalting ourselves when it tells us that God exalts a humble man and resists the proud.[7]

> *Since Paul was a scholar of the Scriptures, it is beyond imagination that he would continually boast of himself and his experiences and yet expect to walk successfully with his God.*

According to God's Word, "Pride goeth before destruction."[8] Therefore, if Paul was filled with pride and boasted of himself, we would expect him to stumble and fall.

From the Word of God, it is clear that Paul understood and rejected any boasting that promoted himself. Instead, we know his boast was in the Lord. We are sure of this, even though he said to the Corinthian church:

---

7 1Pe 5:5-6
8 Pro 16:18

> *Seeing that many glory after the flesh, I will glory also.*[9]

This declaration, obviously tongue-in-cheek, was deliberately stated to expose and counter the deceitful workers who were masquerading as apostles of Christ[10] and boasting about their achievements.[11]

This is apparent when Paul writes:

> *If they can brag, so can I, but it is a foolish thing to do.*[12]

Any other misunderstanding about Paul's boasting is laid aside in his words:

> *When I do all this bragging, I do it as a fool and not for the Lord.*[13]

---

[9] 2Co 11:18
[10] 2Co 11:13 NIV
[11] 2Co 11:12 NLT
[12] 2Co 11:21 CEV
[13] 2Co 11:17 CEV

With this truth pouring from Paul's heart, we are certain he understood the futility of boasting and was not exalting himself. He was simply upending the practice of boasting that prevailed in Corinth [14] and declaring boasting as foolish.

We know this when we hear his words:

> He that glorieth, let him glory in the Lord. [15]

THE MESSENGER OF SATAN

In 2 Corinthians 12:7, Paul makes an interesting statement, often interpreted quite contrary to biblical evidence.

He states:

> Lest I should be exalted above measure through the abundance of the revelations, there was given to me a thorn in the flesh, the messenger of Satan to buffet me.

---

[14] 2Co 11:18, Barnes
[15] 1Co 1:31;2Co 10:17

From this verse, many conclude that God sent a "thorn in the flesh" to Paul because of his pride. They further state that this thorn was a disease. However, if we read this verse carefully, it is clear that **Paul's thorn was not sent by God, and it was not a disease.**

The Scripture definitely states that the "thorn in the flesh" was a messenger of Satan.

This messenger persistently challenged Paul. **To him, Paul was a formidable foe because Paul understood God's great plan of redemption.** In the book of Acts, we note that Satan's messenger constantly pursued Paul, and as a result, Paul was imprisoned, beaten, stoned, and shipwrecked. Because of Paul's many revelations – revelations that would affect cities, states, and countries in every era of time – **Satan's messenger was sent to harass Paul and subvert the gospel of the Lord Jesus Christ.**

The apostle Paul listed many of the difficulties he faced when challenged by the messenger of Satan, but he did NOT mention disease.[16]

---

[16] 2Co 11:23-28;2Ti 3:11

Although many theologians state that Paul had an eye disease, probably some form of ophthalmia, the volume of Scripture does not support this conclusion. From the pen of the apostle Paul himself, there can be no doubt that the messenger of Satan was an angelic being, not a disease.

Any lingering concept of Paul's thorn as a disease is eliminated when we examine the word "messenger" used in this Scripture. This Greek word is used 185 times in the New Testament and is translated angel or angels 178 times and messenger seven times. It always refers to a person or spirit being, never a disease.

> The phrase "thorn in the flesh" is rooted in the Old Testament.

In Numbers 33:55, Israel was instructed to drive out the inhabitants of the land. God said if these inhabitants remained they would vex Israel like pricks in their eyes and thorns in their sides. These pricks – these thorns – were people. Again, in Joshua 23:13, we read of nations that could harass God's people as:

> ...scourges in [their] sides and thorns in [their] eyes.

A thorn in your flesh is an irritant, an aggravation. If

you do not eliminate it promptly, the pain accelerates until you are sure there is a boulder in your eye, although it may simply be a grain of sand. This is the picture Paul draws for us with the terminology "thorn in the flesh." **He is describing a messenger sent by Satan to be a continual antagonist.** This messenger's job was to pressure Paul until he was troubled, distressed, perplexed and destroyed.[17] Today, we use a similar terminology whenever we say irritating people are a "pain in the neck."

GRACE

Now, here is an important question. How can Paul successfully preach the gospel if he is constantly harassed by Satan's angels? The answer given in the Scripture is "by God's grace." Three times Paul asked the Lord to remove this messenger – this thorn – of Satan.

But God said:

> *My grace is sufficient for thee: for my strength is made perfect in weakness.*[18]

---

[17] 2Co 4:8-9
[18] 2Co 12:9

In this verse, **God declared that His grace would be the catalyst of strength** that enabled Paul to overcome weakness.

There is no doubt that Paul needed this strength. When you are beaten, stoned, and imprisoned, there will be injury and pain. Persecution, torment, and buffeting will cause weakness or infirmity. But here is good news! Paul can expect God's strength! The grace of God will send the strength of heaven.

According to the Word of God, the strength of heaven, the power of the risen Christ, would rest upon him.[19] In the Greek language, this means it would cover him like a tent. What a comforting word! Paul could expect the power of God to rest upon him or cover him. Enveloped in God's power, he would overcome every weakness.

This is why Paul said:

When I am weak, then am I strong.[20]

He knew the strength of heaven would rescue him.

So we ask, "Did Paul walk successfully in supernatural strength?" If Paul could answer this question for us in person, I am certain he would remind

---

[19] 2Co 12:9
[20] 2Co 12:10

us of the time he was stoned In Lystra and cast out of the city as dead. As the disciples stood around him, he arose and returned to the city.[21] His weakness was perfected by God's strength!

With this in mind, we can understand Paul's words, "I take pleasure in infirmities."[22]

> *He was content because He knew God's grace would supply overcoming power.*

This power is NOT simply the ability to tolerate difficulties. It is the God-given strength to walk through every work of the enemy.

In 2 Timothy 3:11, Paul declares that he endured persecutions and afflictions at Antioch, Iconium, and Lystra, but he gloriously testifies:

> *Out of them all the Lord delivered me.*

There is no doubt that God worked mightily in Paul's life, leading him to victory with the strength of His Holy Spirit.

Like Paul, we march in God's kingdom, **certain God's grace will perfect our weaknesses.** God's grace is

---

[21] Act 14:19-20;2Ti 3:11
[22] 2Co 12:10

greater than Satan's power! It is greater than every work of the enemy. Therefore we boldly face every obstacle in the power of God's grace. We do not fear because God's grace will bring us through. We are certain!

CHAPTER 9

WHAT ABOUT JOB?

One of the biggest hindrances that prevent those who are sick from receiving the healing power of our mighty God is a misunderstanding of Job's trauma. When we believe Job's difficulties were either the assignment of God, given to Satan for divine purpose, or at least, the work of Satan by divine permission, we thwart any attempt to be healed. These theories cripple man's faith!

A careful study of the book of Job uproots these misconceptions and sets our hearts free from any misunderstanding. Yet **real enlightenment begins when we examine Job through the revelation given in the New Testament.** This is needed because scriptural revelation is progressive.

The further we advance in time, the more man knew about God.

Since scholars tell us Job is the oldest book in the Bible, we know Job did not understand the plans and purposes of God in the same measure as Peter, Paul, or James. The apostle Paul received understanding from the Lord Jesus Christ.[1] He understood the death and Resurrection of our Lord to a far greater extent than was

---

[1] Gal 1:12

possible for Job. His epistle to the Romans explained sin and righteous in light of the cross. This revelation – this knowledge – was concealed in the Old Testament.

The relationship between the Old and the New Testament can be compared to viewing your backyard through frosted glass. Certainly, you can see shapes and outlines, but you cannot see them clearly. But if you open the door, all the details come to light. Our "frosted" view of the Old Testament does not minimize its value or discount the lessons to be learned, but it opens the door of the New Testament to further clarity.

Now, if I had a thorn in my finger, I would not stand in a darkened room to examine it. Instantly, I would go to the greatest source of light. Since the light of the glorious gospel of Christ is most abundant in the New Testament, **we need to examine the life of Job, the works of Satan, and the restoration of Job's blessings with New Testament** revelation.

We do NOT stand in the shadow of the Old Testament to explain the New, but we embrace the New Testament as the revelation of the Old.

One example of the light poured into the Old Testament by the New Testament is found in Job 1:1. This verse declares:

> *There was a man in the land of Uz, whose name was Job; and that man was perfect and upright, and one that feared God, and eschewed evil.*

Here, the Word of God states that Job was "perfect and upright." Today, if we describe something as "perfect," we mean it is "not deficient, defective or faulty."[2] If this is the scriptural meaning, then Job was without sin. Yet, the New Testament says, "For all have sinned,"[3] and this definitely includes Job.

Strong's Hebrew and Greek Dictionary explains this further. Here, the Hebrew word **"perfect"** means to be complete, morally pious, gentle, and dear, and it **stresses integrity.**[4] This assures us that Job was mature, living an honest and upright life. He had great reverence for God and hated evil. However, these wonderful characteristics do NOT declare that Job was a perfect man, without sin.

THE BEGINNING OF TRAUMA

Before Job's overwhelming loss, the "sons of God", or angelic beings, appeared before the Lord and Satan

---

[2] Webster's 1959
[3] Ro 3:23
[4] H8535, Strong's Red Letter

was with them. When God asked Satan:

Where have you come from?[5]

He replied:

From going to and fro in the earth, and from walking up and down in it.

Reading 1 Peter 5:8, we learn that this is Satan's usual agenda. The apostle Peter writes:

Be sober, be vigilant; because your adversary the devil, as a roaring lion, walketh about, seeking whom he may devour.

This verse reveals the purpose of Satan's grand tour of the earth. **He was watching man in order to devour him.**

---

[5] Job 1:7 NLT

In John 10:10, Jesus said:

> *The thief cometh not, but for to steal, and to kill, and to destroy.*

This again highlights the devil's intention. **He plans to KILL and DESTROY.** Then, in John 8:44, we read that he is a MURDERER.

> *These three New Testament Scriptures reveal the heart of our enemy, Satan. He comes to DEVOUR, to KILL, to DESTROY, and to MURDER. He does not come to help man and certainly, he is not an ambassador of our God.*

Our God gives life in great abundance.[6] He is a faithful God, whose mercy endures forever.[7]

It is, therefore, illogical to assume that Satan and God work together. If the objective of Satan is evil and the plan of God is abundant life, then these separate agendas prohibit any interaction between God and the devil. Jesus confirmed this when He said:

---

6 Jn 10:10
7 Lam 3:22-23;Ps 107:1

> *Every kingdom divided against itself is brought to desolation; and every city or house divided against itself shall not stand.*[8]

This verse forfeits any joint effort between God and the devil.

Now, it is interesting to note the second question God asked Satan in the book of Job. He said:

> *Hast thou considered my servant Job, that there is none like him in the earth, a perfect and an upright man, one that feareth God, and escheweth evil?*[9]

At first glance, it appears that God is suggesting Job would be a good candidate for Satan's destruction. However, in the margin of my King James Bible and also in the Literal Translation of the Holy Bible, this question is written:

---

[8] Mt 12:25
[9] Job 1:8

Have you set your heart on my servant Job?

My, what a difference that makes!

When you set your heart on something, you diligently seek it! "Set your heart" on chocolate, and you quickly find a way to appease your desire. You cannot rest until you have chocolate in hand. Well, chocolate is good, but I am a connoisseur of "lemon." I am never without lemon juice in my refrigerator, and "everything lemon" demands my personal attention. If a server does not bring lemon with my tea, I pursue it. I cannot be satisfied without lemon.

The devil had set his heart on Job. He pursued Job in order to DESTROY and DEVOUR him, his family, and all their possessions.

Satan's agenda was evident in God's question to him. He asked Satan, "Have you been watching Job? Have you been thinking about my servant Job?" The devil was watching Job in order to destroy him, and God knew it.

When Satan responded to God's question, he further defined his objective. He wanted Job to curse God. He spoke to God saying, "Touch all that he hath, and he will curse thee to thy face."[10] **Satan wanted Job under so much pressure that he would forfeit his integrity and speak evil of God.** He knew God had blessed Job, but he was sure Job would forget about God if he had great difficulties.

FEAR

The question from the book of Job that has forever plagued Christianity is the matter of the "hedge." When Satan responded to God's second question, he said:

You have made a hedge around Job and all his substance.[11]

The Lord replied:

All that he hath is in thy power.[12]

Some have read God's reply and supposed that God was turning His back on the righteous behavior of His servant, pulling down the hedge to permit Satan's

[10] Job 1:11
[11] Job 1:10, author's paraphrase
[12] Job 1:12

destruction. Yet **this is contrary to the nature of our life-giving Father.**

When Abraham stood before God to plead the cause of Sodom, he boldly asked God:

Wilt thou [God] also destroy the righteous with the wicked?"[13]

He continued:

That be far from thee to do after this manner, to slay the righteous with the wicked.[14]

I am certain that the God of Abraham who answered Abraham's cry to protect the righteous in Sodom is also the God of Job. **He would not arbitrarily remove His hand of protection at Satan's suggestion.**

In the Scripture, a hedge is symbolic of the protection and blessings of God. Deuteronomy 28 notes that these benefits came to Israel when they were obedient to God's commands. Therefore, the hedge

---

[13] Ge 18:23
[14] Ge 18:25

around Israel **was contingent on their obedience.** If Israel was obedient to the Lord, they were plenteous in goods and the enemy was afraid of them.[15]

In the book of Job, we quickly discern God's hedge of protection was no longer secure in Job's life. When God said to Satan, "All that he [Job] hath is in thy power,"[16] He was not opening the door to satanic attack, **but revealing Job's present condition.**

One significant reason for Job's vulnerability to Satan's destructive power was fear. In Job 3:25, Job said:

The thing which I greatly feared is come upon me, and that which I was afraid of is come unto me.

If we pour the light of the New Testament into this admission of fear, we hear the apostle Paul declares:

God hath not given us the spirit of fear.[17]

---

[15] Deu 28:1-14
[16] Job 1:12
[17] 2Ti 1:7

Fear is not from God; therefore, **fear is an important factor in the cause of Job's dilemma**.

Job's fear is apparent in his continual sacrifices for his children. He offered burnt sacrifices for his children because he had decided:

It MAY BE that my sons have sinned, and cursed God in their hearts."[18]

This is a powerful indication of the size of Job's fear—fear he did not deny. Again, Job said:

The thing which I greatly feared is come upon me, and that which I was afraid of is come unto me.

One cannot read this statement without understanding that long before his great loss, **Job had pondered the possibility of disaster**.

Despite this, and despite Satan's brutal attack which destroyed Job's cattle, his servants and his children, Job's integrity remained.

---

[18] Job 1:5, author's emphasis

The Scripture records:

In all this Job sinned not, nor charged God foolishly.[19]

Remember, Satan's objective was to cause Job to curse God, but in this he failed. In spite of his pain and loss, Job did not blaspheme God. In fact, he bowed to the ground and worshipped.[20] Satan did not win!

INADEQUATE KNOWLEDGE AND REVELATION

The New Testament states the prevailing lesson to be learned from the book of Job when it says:

Ye have heard of the patience of Job, and have seen the end of the Lord; that the Lord is very pitiful, and of tender mercy."[21]

This verse encourages us to concentrate on Job's

---

[19] Job 1:22
[20] Job 1:20
[21] Jas 5:11

patience and endurance. According to the apostle James, **Job's patience and God's mercy should be at the forefront of our thinking**, not Job's suffering.

Strong's Hebrew and Greek Dictionary defines the word "patience" as "cheerful (or hopeful) endurance, constancy." It is "the temper which does not easily succumb under suffering." [22] What a wonderful description of Job! **In spite of earth-shaking trauma, he held fast to God and worshipped Him.** He was patient and walked in the light of the revelation he possessed.

However, Job's knowledge about God and his understanding of his present suffering were meager. Numerous statements recorded in the book of Job highlight this lack of knowledge. One example is given in Job 3:23 when Job asked:

Why is life given to those with no future, those God has surrounded with difficulties?[23]

From the New Testament, we learn that:

---

[22] G5281, Strong's Red Letter
[23] NLT, Biblegateway.com

> *God cannot be tempted with evil, neither tempteth he any man.*[24]

Further, we read:

> *Every good gift and every perfect gift is from above."*[25]

Since Job's circumstances were not good or perfect, **we know they did not come from God**, our Father. Job simply did not understand that God does not surround us with evil.

Another misunderstanding Job had is revealed in his declaration to his friends. He said:

> *Innocent or wicked, it is all the same to God. That's why I say, 'He destroys both the blameless and the wicked.'*[26]

---

[24] Jas 1:13
[25] Jas 1:17
[26] Job 9:22 NLT, Biblegateway.com

Throughout the Old and New Testament, there is abundant evidence that this statement is wrong. In 2 Peter 2:6, we learn that Sodom and Gomorrah were condemned because they lived a godless life. Their choice brought judgment into their lives. This same chapter testifies that Lot was a righteous man delivered from Sodom's destruction and brought to safety by the intervention of God. Clearly, God does not destroy both the blameless and the wicked.

> *Man is destroyed by his own choice, not by the selection of God.*

Jesus proved this when He said:

> *He that believeth on [the Son of God] is not condemned: but he that believeth not is condemned already, because he hath not believed in the name of the only begotten Son of God."*[27]

It is obvious from this verse **that man is condemned because he rejects Jesus as Savior and Lord**.

Other Scriptures also emphasize the consequence

---

[27] Jn 3:18

of man's choice. Deuteronomy 30:19 states:

> I call heaven and earth to record this
> day against you, that I have set before
> you life and death, blessing and
> cursing: therefore choose life, that
> both thou and thy seed may live.

THE RESTORATION OF JOB

There were many other words spoken by Job and his friends that were incorrect, but Job recognized this when God spoke to him out of a whirlwind.

God asked Job:

> Who is this that questions my wisdom
> with such ignorant words?[28]

The New Jerusalem Bible says, "empty-headed words," and the Knox Translation includes the words "clouding the truth." These Bible scholars greatly enhance our understanding.

Challenged by God's truth, Job bowed his heart in

---

[28] Job 38:2 NLT

deep contrition, acknowledging his ignorance, and said:

> *"I am nothing – how could I ever find the answers? I will cover my mouth with my hand. I have said too much already. I have nothing more to say."*[29]

For the first time, Job acknowledged his misguided thinking. What wonderful words of repentance! Job declared:

> *I was talking about things I knew nothing about.*[30]

And

> *I abhor myself, and repent in dust and ashes.*[31]

---

[29] Job 40:4-5 NLT, Biblegateway.com
[30] Job 42:3 NLT, Biblegateway.com
[31] Job 42:6

Job is a great example because he listened to God and admitted his sin. He had spoken many inaccurate words, but finally he said the one phrase that brought freedom and restoration. He said, "I repent." **It was this word**, not Job's previous words, that God held out to Job's friends as right.

CAPTIVITY ENDED

After Job repented, "God blessed Job's later life even more than his earlier life."[32] God magnificently delivered him from every trauma, every loss, releasing him from Satanic bondage.

> *God always rescues us from sin, sickness, and poverty if we trust in Him.*

Jesus was anointed by God to set captives free, not destroy them. He was a reflection of His Father's purpose to bring deliverance and freedom to all who would believe.

Now, according to Bible scholars, Job's difficulties took place in a few months.[33] Yet people have examined and magnified these months until they hide the glory of Job's recovery. After Job repented and prayed for his

---

[32] Job 42:12 MSG
[33] "Job–Biblical Data", Jewish Enc.

friends, God blessed him with ten children and twice as many goods as he previously owned.[34] His health was restored, and he lived to enjoy four generations of his family.

> *This is the will of God for us today. He wants to bless His children. He wants us to "prosper and be in health, even as [our] soul prospers."[35]*

Yet in the past, many have believed God wants us to suffer. But now, we understand Job's trauma, and we know God wants us to be free – free like His servant Job. Job is no longer an explanation of our bondage, but a declaration of our freedom. The truth about Job has set us free! Free indeed! AMEN!

---

[34] Job 42:10
[35] 3Jn 1:2

CHAPTER 10

THE CHASTENING OF THE LORD

For many years, I circumvented any study on the subject of God's chastening because I supposed I might live more peacefully in ignorance. I did not understand the merciful nature of our God, so I was sure He would chasten me with sickness or some other evil, and I just thought I was better off not knowing. Oh, how wrong I was!

Over the years, chastening has earned a very bad reputation because it has been expanded to include accidents, illness, great loss, and number of devastating events. According to many, these catastrophes are designed to teach us valuable lessons. But when we walk in the light of the Scripture, we know this cannot be true.

The Word of God testifies that:

...the thief comes only to steal and kill and destroy."[1]

Certainly, **God is not a thief, and He does not intervene in our lives through disaster.** Satan, the thief, comes with his arsenal of weapons, and he orchestrates

---

[1] Jn 10:10 NIV

these overwhelming dilemmas that upend us.

The testimony of James proves God never chastens us with evil. In James 1:13, he declares:

God cannot be tempted by evil, and he doesn't use evil to tempt others."[2]

He also writes:

Every good action and every perfect gift is from God.[3]

Well, we know **sickness is not good or perfect**. In fact, in our previous studies, we learned that it oppresses and tyrannizes man, binding him and imprisoning him. It is evil and, therefore, it cannot come from our great and mighty God.

According to the psalmist, God is a good God who does good things.[4] Given that fact, **it is impossible for Him to use sickness or any other evil to correct us** and re-direct our lives.

---

[2] Jas 1:13 CEV
[3] Jas 1:17 NCV
[4] Ps 119:68, author's paraphrase

Yet, He does chasten us. But, how does He chasten us?

WHAT IS CHASTENING?

In our Greek concordance, the word "chastening" means education, training, instruction, and discipline.[5] In Hebrews 12:5, this educational and disciplinary process is referenced as a word of exhortation or rebuke. The King James Version says:

And ye have forgotten the exhortation which speaketh unto you as unto children, My son, despise not thou the chastening of the Lord, nor faint when thou art rebuked of him.

Here, we note the words "exhortation" and "rebuke." However, in the GOD'S WORD translation, we read, "You have forgotten the encouraging words that God speaks to you as His children." This version expands our horizons further by referring to an exhortation as "encouraging words." The New Living Translation also says, "Encouraging words."

With this in mind, we know that chastening is not a

---

[5] G3809, Strong's Red Letter

disease. There isn't anything about a disease that encourages us. In fact, if we are certain sickness is imminent, we are discouraged. But Bible scholars declare that **chastening words are encouraging words.** They are words of comfort, but they are also words of warning.

> *Chastening is a rebuke that educates us so that we can make necessary corrections.*

They are **words that help us**, not words designed to bring great agony and pain.

Hebrews 12:7 declares that God speaks these encouraging words to His sons. Now, no loving father corrects his son by giving him a disease or orchestrating tragedy in his life. This type of behavior is illegal and unconscionable and would lead to his arrest. However, isn't it amazing that we think God could be this heartless and cruel?

> *God, our Father, corrects us because He loves us and wants us to successfully reach the end of life's race.*

He wants to greet us saying, "Well done, thou good

and faithful servant."[6]

A WORD OF CORRECTION

In Hebrews, we are instructed to reverence our Father when He corrects us and to "endure" His chastening or rebuke. This may sound harsh, but here the word "endure" means to be patient, to persevere, or as we might say, to hang in there.[7] Again, we are not talking about harsh treatment and tragedy.

> *The Scripture is simply counselling us to hear the word of the Lord, to listen to His correction, and then to OBEY Him.*

Now, I don't know anyone who enjoys correction, but it is the finest thing that can happen if we are on the wrong road. When God comes to us saying, "You have made a mistake. This needs to be corrected," for the moment, we may be grieved.

Yet, instead of sorrow or despair, we ought to shout at the top of our lungs. "Now, I know what to do. I know where I was wrong. I know what to change." What a glorious revelation chastening can bring to us.

For me, this truth is not simply a theory! Over a

---

[6] Mt 25:21
[7] G5278, Strong's

period of two weeks, many years ago, I struggled to teach with little anointing, seemingly backed into a corner. Eventually, I was in such despair that I asked someone to pray for me. They quickly discerned an area in my life that needed to be corrected. I had made a commitment that I regretted, and I ignored this obligation for a long time, deciding I wasn't going to do it. Once some time had passed, it became erased from my memory, and I totally forgot it.

The psalmist asks the question, "O Lord, who shall stay in Thy tabernacle?"[8] His answer to this query includes, "He that sweareth to his own hurt, and changeth not."[9] The Modern Language Bible says, "Though swearing to his own detriment, [he] does not change." The Message Bible simply declares, "Keep your word even when it costs you." I mention this verse of Scripture because it was very familiar to me and should have guided my decisions. But it did not. The dilemma I found myself in was **not propagated by ignorance, but by disobedience**.

It was a wonderful, wonderful day when I realized my mistake. Quickly, I fulfilled my obligation, and now, I do not give my word lightly. When I say, "I will," I keep my word.

As God's children, we heed His correction. He is our Father, and we submit to Him. When we obey Him, the

---

[8] Ps 15:1 MLB
[9] Ps 15:4

Scripture decrees that **it will be profitable for us.**[10] This means that it is **to our advantage.** It makes things better for us.

The Contemporary English Version ably explains:

> God corrects us for our own good, because he wants us to be holy, as he is.[11]

The New Century Version writes:

> God disciplines us to help us, so we can become holy as he is.

Through God's words of correction, God guides our behavior so that we can live in righteousness and peace.[12]

HEAR AND OBEY

Because God corrects us and we obey, we walk on the right path in His strength. Just as the Scripture has

---

[10] Heb 12:9-10
[11] Heb 12:10
[12] Heb 12:11

promised, we are not weak, feeble, lame, or disabled. We are able to finish our race in the will of God, invigorated by the power of heaven.

However, according to the writer of Hebrews, we must patiently run this race, laying aside every sin and weight from our lives.[13]

> *Sin and weights will prevent us from getting to the goal line.*

A weight is any burden or hindrance that thwarts our success.

When Wayne was in the military, his unit ran approximately one mile in heavy boots every morning. Yet boots are not the proper gear for a racetrack. Heavy shoes would be a hindrance there. They are weights and must be removed. Similarly, when we travel overseas in the winter time, we carry sweaters, coats, and fur-lined boots. But in Florida, these are put away because they would be a burden in the heat.

Years ago, tennis was a weight to me, a hindrance, and a barrier to what God wanted for my life. When God began to deal with me to stop playing, I argued with Him, saying, "It's really good exercise." Then I added, "It's really the only exercise I get and I'm only gone a couple of hours." I tried to talk God into a compromise,

---

[13] Heb 12:1

but I couldn't make a deal with Him. That never works. So finally, I gave up tennis.

Now, there is absolutely nothing wrong with tennis. However, if I had continued to play tennis, I would have been disobedient, and eventually, it would have subverted God's purpose for my life. God asked me to forget about myself, lay tennis aside, and concentrate on Him. Of course, this word to me does not mean that you can't play tennis. An obstacle that hinders me is not a barrier to you. God guides each of us differently. Regardless, sin is wrong for all of us.

A SUCCESSFUL RACE

God wants us to finish our race **successfully** so He deals with us, enabling us to identify any obstacles and remove them. If we heed His words, we do not run life's race weighted down by boots and an overcoat. This is the profound impact of Hebrews 12. In verse 1, we are on the starting line of God's race, aware that wrong decisions will hinder us. But quickly, the Word of God assures us that God will chasten us, correct us, and discipline us so that we can recognize and overcome every obstacle.

Each word of chastening illuminates a path that accomplishes the will and purpose of God.

These words position us for victory. However, we

must, again, note that if we do not follow God's direction, we will experience great loss. When we do not heed His voice and eliminate sins and weights, their heavy burden will cause us to live as one who is lame. The writer of Hebrews declares that our lame feet will be "turned out of the way," or, as the New King James' says, "dislocated." [14] What a graphic description of failure!

Yet there is good news! "Instead of getting worse," we can become stronger. We can:

...stand up straight! Stop [our] knees from shaking and walk a straight path." [15]

But this is only possible if we allow God to lead us. We **must constantly submit to His words of instruction** and, through these words, successfully "run the race that is set before us." [16]

For this reason, we cherish the chastening of the Lord. Whenever we are confused and perplexed, lacking direction, we cry out, "Lord, chasten us!" We know He does NOT send sickness and disease, but instead, He

---

[14] Heb 12:12-13, author's paraphrase
[15] Heb 12:12-13 CEV
[16] Heb 12:1, author's emphasis

teaches us and corrects us through His Word. With His Word in our heart, we can navigate every difficulty. What a wonderful Father! We can depend on Him!

SECTION 3

NO MORE RELUCTANCE

Jesus said unto him, If thou canst believe, all things are possible to him that believeth (Mk 9:23).

CHAPTER 11

THE BRIDGE OF FAITH

Over forty years ago, we built our home on property deeded to us by my husband's father. Because there is a canal that crosses the front of the property, we constructed a bridge and built our home toward the back. Today, when we give directions to our home, we tell people to "take the asphalt drive and cross the bridge." You must cross the bridge to get to our house.

> *In the Scripture, faith is the bridge that carries us to the blessings of God.*

On one side of the bridge is God's legal provision — those things purchased by the death of our Lord. On the other side is the manifestation of that provision. This, we'll call the experiential side. Through the Word of God we learn what has been legally provided for us. Then **with our faith, we travel from this legal provision to experience God's bounty.**

Before my father died, he made legal provision for his three children. In advance, he signed every document that would give us his home and various monetary accounts. After he went to be with the Lord, this provision was ours. First, it was legally ours, and then we possessed it.

Through Jesus Christ, God has bountifully provided for us. In Romans 8:32, we read:

He that spared not his own Son, but delivered him up for us all, how shall he not with him also freely give us all things?

Here, we note the legal provision that God made for man when Jesus died for us. **Through Jesus' death, God has provided us with ALL things.**

What a tremendous word, ALL. We cannot compromise its meaning or water it down. It does not mean some things, a few things, or even many things. ALL means ALL, and certainly, this includes healing from every sickness and disease.

THE PAST TENSE OF GOD'S WORD

In Ephesians 1:3 the apostle Paul writes:

Blessed be the God and Father of our Lord Jesus Christ, who hath blessed us with all spiritual blessings in heavenly places in Christ.

Here, again, we note the word ALL. However, many

Bible translations say, "EVERY spiritual blessing."[1]

In Webster's New Collegiate Dictionary, the word "every" is defined as:

each (individual or part), without exception; complete; entire.

Now, for the second time, we know that **every blessing must include healing for the body and mind.**

In this verse, we also notice the word BLESSED. Because it is past tense, we cannot say, "God will bless us in the future." Through Jesus Christ, He has already blessed us, and today, we are expecting the manifestation of this blessing. Similarly, in 1 Peter 2:24 we read:

*By whose stripes ye **were** healed.*

Here again, the past tense verb "were" confirms that the bounty of heaven is now legally provided.

God's past-tense blessing provided by the death and resurrection of our Lord is easily understood when we consider the new birth. Often, when we pray for

---

[1] NAS, NIV, NLT, NKJV, author's emphasis

someone who is not born again, we petition God to "save them" without remembering that He has already legally provided salvation. Yet through the death of His Son, the work of salvation is finished. Jesus died many years ago, and salvation is now available.

The problem is that they do not understand God's gracious gift of His Son, or they have chosen to reject the glorious gospel of our salvation. Therefore, we correctly pray and ask God to give them revelation of what He has already done for them through Jesus Christ. As they gain knowledge of God's saving Word, the Holy Spirit draws them to the Father and convicts them of sin. Then they can experience what has been legally provided by declaring Jesus as their Savior and Lord. But again, we are reminded that the plan of salvation was completed many centuries before they accepted it. It was through their faith that they accessed this great blessing of God.

THE BRIDGE OF FAITH

Every aspect of God's legal provision is received by faith before it manifests in our lives. We can't get from the legal side of God's provision to the experience of that provision without the support of faith. Years ago, the supports of our bridge collapsed after a delivery truck crossed it. The top structure was sound, but no one could cross the bridge until the support system was repaired. In like manner, we must secure and maintain our faith in order to receive God's abundant blessing.

Faith knows what God has provided and boldly accepts it by speaking His Word.

This declaration of faith doesn't demand proof from the physical senses. **We speak because we believe** in the work of the cross and the shed blood of Jesus. We speak because we know God does not lie and He said that we were healed. Legally, it is ours in the same manner a will guarantees our children's' inheritance. The will, when written and signed, assures that your family will enjoy everything you had planned for them. Although, you may live many years after the document is recorded, today, it is legal. Then, at your death, everything you left for your heirs will manifest in their lives.

But, here is the good news! We are not waiting for Jesus to die so that we can enjoy the promises of God's Word. The Word of God is the Last Will and Testament of our Lord Jesus Christ, and **after Jesus died and rose from the dead, the benefits of this Last Will were available.**[2] This does not mean that God's bounty will instantly or immediately manifest in our lives.

I love the word "immediately," but I have learned that, often, faith's blessings come to us progressively.

---

[2] Heb 9:16-17

Our part is to **plant the seed of the Word in our heart and water it continually.** When a farmer plants his field with seed, he expects a harvest even though there is no immediate evidence. He believes the seed is sprouting, and in his heart, he envisions much fruit.

CONFIDENCE IN GOD

We must not "cast away" our confidence in God and His Word. A devastating diagnosis or trauma, pain or unexpected medical procedures frequently urge us to surrender in fear. But God is a wonderful Father, who remains faithful to His Word. Our confidence in Him "will be richly rewarded."[3] So do not quit!

> *Do not give up or surrender, but steadily embrace the mighty provision of the cross – God's legal provision – knowing that you will experience a great harvest.*

Everything God legally bestowed will manifest in your life as you keep walking the bridge of faith.

The bridge of faith is secured by the forever-settled Word of God.[4] It is not like a swinging bridge that vibrates with every footstep. As a child, we lived

---

[3] Heb 10:35 NIV
[4] Ps 119:89

near a tourist attraction and walked across its swinging bridge. Certainly you felt unsettled as it swayed from left to right. However, **faith is steadfast and immoveable.** It is anchored and established in God's Word, which testifies:

There hath not failed one word of all his good promise.[5]

Therefore, trust God! Trust His Word! He has abundantly provided!

---

[5] 1Ki 8:56

CHAPTER 12

FAITH WORKS

I know you have heard the oft-expressed sentiment, "God is in control." It is usually uttered in the most horrendous situations, and, although it is true when properly understood, its frequent misapplication causes my heart to cringe. When someone says, "If God wants it to happen, it will," I know they don't understand the God-given role faith plays in every victory and are instead relying solely on God to do everything for them.

We must not leave the impression that man has no responsibility, and consequently, no choice through the ups and downs of life.

> *Faith, a necessary component for prosperity and success, is idle and ineffective if we believe that every life experience depends on God alone.*

Our faith makes a difference! Although God can and often does take the initiative, He also decrees:

> *"If thou canst believe, all things are possible to him that believeth."*[1]

---

[1] Mk 9:23

Our great and mighty Father honors faith. Yet when the apostle Paul wrote about the gifts, or manifestations, of God's Spirit, he said God would divide them "to every man severally as He will."[2] This means that we cannot order God to send us a gift. We can wait on a gift, or manifestation, but it may not come. God decides! But this does not leave us without hope. Remember? **God has promised that all things are possible if we believe.**

Years ago, a gentleman told me about an injury to his knee. By his own admission, he came to church believing that his pastor would pray for people who had injured their knees. When it didn't happen right away, he refused to be discouraged and came to several more services knowing that God would speak to the pastor about knees. Yet that never happened. Finally, as he was actually limping to his car after church, he boldly said, "I believe I am healed. God said so," and in that moment, his knee was completely healed. All that time, he had waited on a gift, which comes as God wills, instead of walking in faith.

> *Faith depends on the promises of God and leans on the work of the cross. It functions for everyone.*

---

[2] 1Co 12:11

The apostle Paul confirmed this marvelous truth saying:

He that spared not his own Son, but delivered him up for us all, how shall he not with him also freely give us all things?[3]

I love the terminology, "us all." Jesus died for US ALL and through His death "all things" are freely given to us.

This all-inclusive nature of the gospel was identified when Jesus directed the disciples to "teach all nations."[4] The gospel of Mark records that they were to preach the good news to "every creature."[5] The New Living Translation says, "To everyone, everywhere." The Message Bible writes to:

...announce the Message of God's good news to one and all.

---

[3] Rm 8:32
[4] Mt 28:19
[5] Mk 16:15

Without any doubt, **the vast benefits of the gospel are for everyone.** We can ask God for any of these benefits and know that He will honor our request.

Jesus said:

Whatever things you ask when you pray, believe that you receive them, and you will have them.[6]

In the Contemporary English Version, this verse reads:

Everything you ask for in prayer will be yours, if you only have faith.

The New Century Version says:

Believe that you have received the things you ask for in prayer, and God will give them to you.

---

[6] Mk 11:24 NKJV

What a magnificent declaration from our Lord Jesus Christ. **When we ask in faith, every heavenly blessing will be ours.** Provided for us through the death and Resurrection of our Lord, our faith makes them available.

FAITH FOR HEALING

Faith is the foundation of salvation and all of its benefits. Healing for our bodies and our minds is one of those heavenly benefits, and faith is the vehicle that transports it into our lives. Faith in God brings healing power to us.

This important union of faith and healing power is particularly highlighted in the ministry of Jesus. In the gospel of Matthew, two blind men came to Jesus crying out for mercy. Jesus asked them:

"Do you believe that I am able to do this?"[7]

In essence, His question was, "Do you have faith in me?"

When they responded, "Yes, Lord,"[8] Jesus touched their eyes.

---

[7] Mt 9:28 NKJV
[8] Mt 9:28 NKJV

He said:

"According to your faith be it unto you."[9]

Their eyes were opened, and because of their faith, they were healed.

At another time, a centurion came to Jesus because his servant was very ill. With great faith, the centurion said to Jesus:

"Speak the word only, and my servant shall be healed."[10]

Jesus commended his faith, saying:

"I haven't seen faith like this in all the land of Israel."[11]

---

[9] Mt 9:29
[10] Mt 8:8
[11] Mt 8:10 NLT

Through the centurion's faith, his servant was healed that same hour.[12]

Again, a nobleman, whose son was close to death, came to Jesus asking Him to go to his son's bedside. Jesus did not go with him, but instead, He said:

"Go your way; your son lives."[13]

The Scripture records:

The man believed the word that Jesus had spoken unto him, and he went his way.[14]

As he was traveling home, his servants met him with the good news, "Your son lives."[15] Obviously, every step toward home was a step of faith.

In each of these instances, **faith was the catalyst of healing and health.** As we study the Scripture, we quickly note that faith is the most frequent agent of

---

[12] Mt 8:13
[13] Jn 4:50 NKJV
[14] Jn 4:50
[15] Jn 4:51 NKJV

healing power. Of course, some are healed by a gift of the Spirit, but **faith is the primary method of healing** recorded in the Word of God.

The woman with the issue of blood is a great example of healing by faith. She received the healing power of God, called *virtue*,[16] after she touched Jesus' clothes. We know that she touched Him by faith because she said:

> "If I can just touch his clothing, I will be healed."[17]

Because of her faith, God's power poured into her body and she was well.

Now, it is interesting that Jesus did not attribute her healing and recovery to HIS faith or to HIS power. He said:

> "Daughter, thy faith hath made thee whole."[18]

---

[16] G1411, Strong's
[17] Mk 5:28 NLT
[18] Mk 5:34

Similar words were spoken after the two blind men were healed. Jesus said:

"According to your faith be it unto you."[19]

There is no doubt that their faith accessed God's healing power.

GIFTS OF HEALINGS

Faith always works. But in addition to faith, we have the wonder of gifts of healings. It is one of the nine manifestations of the Spirit listed by the apostle Paul in 1 Corinthians 12, and, as previously mentioned, all of them work as the Spirit wills.

One person rescued by the gifts of healings was the man at the pool of Bethesda. This man had been sick for thirty-eight years, and, although the angel of the Lord periodically stirred the waters of the pool and the first one in was healed, he was never able to enter and receive his healing. Then one day, Jesus came to him asking, "Do you want to be made well?"[20]

The man's response immediately revealed that He did not expect to be healed. He said, "Sir, I have no man

[19] Mt 9:29
[20] Jn 5:6 NKJV

to put me into the pool when the water is stirred up."[21]

> *Although the man did not have faith to be healed, Jesus said, "Rise, take up they bed, and walk."[22]*

This man did not know who had commanded him to walk. However, he was healed! He was healed by the gifts of healings that, like all the manifestations, are distributed as the Holy Spirit determines.[23]

The question of many hearts is, "Why did God heal this man when he did not exercise faith to be healed? Why did God manifest this healing gift?" I can only guess. One thing I have learned after many years of teaching is not to answer a question when God has not spoken. So in these cases, we are not ashamed to say, "I don't know." Our omniscient Father always does what is best!

WALK BY FAITH

This leaves us with a new question. What should we do when no gift of the Spirit manifests to help us? The answer is very simple. **We walk by faith!** In fact, we always walk by faith.

---

[21] Jn 5:7 NKJV
[22] Jn 5:8
[23] 1Co 12:11, NIV, author's paraphrase

Throughout the Word of God, we are instructed, "The just shall live by faith."[24]

The apostle Paul emphasized this great truth, saying:

We walk by faith, not by sight."[25]

This very important decree guides our lives, especially as we seek the healing power of heaven for our body and mind. **We are healed because we have faith in God.**

These are the words of Jesus. He counseled His disciples to "have faith in God."[26] He further declared:

"If you have faith in God and don't doubt, you can tell this mountain to get up and jump into the sea, and it will."[27]

---

[24] Hab 2:4;Ro 1:17;Gal 3:11;Heb 10:38
[25] 2Co 5:7
[26] Mk 11:22
[27] Mk 11:23 CEV

I love His statement, "It will." He did not say, "It might," or "I hope." He said, "It will."

In like manner, the gospel of Matthew records:

Ask, and it will be given to you.[28]

Jesus gives great emphasis to this promise when He adds, "Everyone that asks receives."[29]

Now, I know it is utterly ridiculous to ask, but does "everyone" include you? People often stumble here and somehow decide they could be excluded. However, there is no reason for that conclusion. When Jesus testified of His death and Resurrection, He said that WHOSOEVER believed in Him would receive eternal life.[30]

The apostle Paul also testified:

WHOSOEVER shall call upon the name of the Lord shall be saved.[31]

---

[28] Mt 7:7 NKJV
[29] Mt 7:8 Darby
[30] Jn 3:16, author's emphasis
[31] Ro 10:13, author's emphasis

Like the songwriter so ably said, "'Whosoever' meaneth me."[32] Salvation is for WHOSOEVER. What glorious words – whosoever, everyone, me!

> *God's plan to heal our physical bodies*
> *is also for WHOSOEVER.*

It is for EVERYONE who believes that the blood-stained cross and the empty tomb brought freedom from sin and sickness. If we read the experiences of Israel at Passover or study the sacrificial law of Leviticus, our hearts cannot escape this truth. The prophetic writings of Isaiah and the inspiration of the psalmist again prove this fact. Repeatedly, the Old Testament speaks of healing through the cross of our Lord.

The New Testament also states that we are healed through the sacrifice of Jesus. From Matthew's gospel to John's vision in Revelation, we learn that EVERYONE who believes in Jesus' death for sin and disease can be healed. Through the cross, healing is ours! What a wonderful Savior! We are so grateful that the sacrifice of our Lord Jesus Christ delivered us from sin and disease.

---

[32] Song1

CHAPTER 13

FAITH SPEAKS

The Scripture declares:

Faith comes by hearing, and hearing by the word of God."[1]

What an important truth! Faith comes through the Word of God, and the apostle Paul says it comes "by hearing, and hearing."[2] As we continually hear God's Word, it fills our heart, enabling us to access the blessings of heaven. Certainly, healing is one of those blessings. Through Jesus' death and Resurrection, it is provided for us, but we must accept it with our faith.

Now, this phrase — "faith comes" — is very interesting. It reminds me of the many times we have waited for a package to arrive at our home and office. We keep looking out the window and down the driveway, expecting the delivery truck because we know the package will come. Similarly, when a child expects Grandma to visit, he watches for her. He knows that she is coming.

This important relationship of faith and hearing is

---

[1] Rm 10:17 NKJV
[2] Rm 10:17

easily understood when we study the Scripture. The household of Cornelius was saved and filled with the Holy Spirit as Peter was preaching. They heard God's words, and their faith brought salvation and the gift of the Holy Spirit.[3] In the City of Samaria, Philip preached about Christ. As a result, the people heard and believed in the name of Jesus.[4] At Ephesus, Paul explained John's message of repentance and taught about Jesus. They believed his message and were baptized.[5]

All these people heard God's Word and then believed its message.

FAITH AND ACTION

God's Word always makes faith available, but as faith comes, the hearer must actively respond to God's truth. In the book of James, it is written:

Faith, if it hath not works, is dead, being alone.[6]

Because of this epistle's frequent references to "my brethren," we know that this verse is written to every

---

[3] Act 10:44-48
[4] Act 8:5-12
[5] Act 19:1-6
[6] Jas 2:17

Christian, not to sinners receiving the new birth.[7] In the book of Ephesians, the apostle Paul states definitely that salvation is received by grace through faith:

Not of works, lest any man should boast.[8]

Therefore, we know that the works of faith mentioned in the book of James are the works of believers.

From this verse in James, we learn that hearing is only the beginning of faith. After we have heard God's promise or command, we acknowledge our faith through our actions.

For instance, Abraham prepared to offer Isaac on the altar because God had spoken to him. His action was based on the Word of the Lord.[9] Again, Rahab and her household were saved from destruction because she followed the directions given to her by Israel's

---

[7] Jas 1:2,16,19; Jas 2:1,5,14; Jas 3:1,10,12; Jas 4:11; Jas 5:9-10, 12, 19
[8] Eph 2:8-9
[9] Jas 2:21-23

messengers.[10] She acted on God's specific instructions given to her by the spies.

> *Without action, faith is dead, ineffective, and lifeless.*

According to the apostle James, this kind of faith is futile and can be compared to physical death.[11] Just as we do not expect an earthly response from one who is deceased, we will not be profited by faith without accompanying deeds. Similarly, a destitute brother or sister is not profited by words alone.[12] Action is required before their need is met.

FAITH AND WORDS

This, of course, does not overlook or minimize the importance of words.

> *In fact, words are the first response of faith.*

The salvation, healing, and deliverance that God has provided are accepted by verbally declaring the Word of the Lord. The apostle Paul shares this revelation in

---

[10] Jas 2:25; Jos 2:18-21; Jos 6:17,25
[11] Jas 2:26
[12] Jas 2:14-16

Romans 10:9-10. He states:

> *If you confess with your mouth that Jesus is Lord and believe in your heart that God has raised Him from the dead, you will be saved.*[13]

Therefore, after we hear and believe that God raised Jesus from the dead, we acknowledge Him as Savior and Lord with our words.

This same principle is explained to the church at Corinth when the apostle Paul declared:

> *We having the same spirit of faith, according as it is written, I believed, and therefore have I spoken.*[14]

Once again, we confirm that faith believes the Word of God and speaks the Word of God. With our words of faith, we confess what God has said to us. Without confession, faith is incomplete.

In the Greek language, the word "confession"

---

[13] NLT
[14] 2Co 4:13

means "to speak the same thing," or to assent, acknowledge, and agree with another.[15] This definition confirms **that our words must agree with God's Word.** In spite of this truth, we can turn from God's promises and agree with Satan's words of destruction.

It is so easy to repeat the devil's negative report and speak his words.

But the more we speak Satan's words, the more we believe them.

Satan's words are devastating. He says, "You look awful," even when you feel well. If you are limping, he declares that the injury is permanent. He reports that your headache is life-threatening, being quick to say, "It's a brain tumor, and no one can help you." In every dilemma, he loudly decrees, "You will never get better." But, we cannot, we must not listen to him.

We must hear, believe, and speak the Word of God.

Healing and every blessing of heaven come to us when we believe, speak, and act on God's Word.

---

[15] G3670, Strong's Red Letter

GOD FULFILLS HIS WORD

In Jeremiah 1:12, God says:

> *"I will hasten my word to perform it."*

In the Complete Bible, an American Translation, this verse reads:

> *"I am watching over my word to put it into effect."*

This assures us that our great and mighty God is active and alert, watching over His Word to fulfill every promise. **Through our acts and words of faith, He brings them to pass.** For this reason, we should not hesitate to boldly and joyfully declare His Word. We know He will do what He said.[16]

Even so, sometimes we are reluctant to speak God's promises. This should never be! When men believe in a football team, they loudly extol its victory. It doesn't matter that they probably cannot win. They enthusiastically, unrelentingly decree success. If you are

---

[16] Lk 1:45 NLT

not a sports fan, you may tire of their continual chatter, but they believe in the team and cannot be silenced.

Similarly, I once visited a friend, who was baking a cake, and she could not be silenced. She asked me if I had ever used that particular recipe, but when I said no, she could not say enough about it. She was sure her recipe was far better than the one I used, so she continually promoted it. Finally, I asked her to write it down for me.

When we passionately embrace a person, product, or idea, no one has to urge us to "speak up". Instead, the people around us hope we will change the subject. This is usually impossible! Our enthusiasm continues to show through our words and actions.

> *Because we believe in the Word of God, we also passionately and eagerly claim His promises.*

It is not a chore, nor do we feel obligated to declare His truth. Automatically, the Word of God pours from our heart. We believe, therefore, we speak.[17]

THE LAW OF FAITH

We confirm our trust in God by our words and our acts of faith. When they correspond to God's promises,

---

[17] 2Co 4:13, author's paraphrase

His blessings are established in our lives. This is the law of faith. We believe; we speak, and we actively respond.

> *Prayer, praise, and thanksgiving are the primary acts of faith.*

When Paul and Silas were in prison, they prayed and sang praises to God.[18] From the belly of a great fish, Jonah prayed, saying:

> *"I will sacrifice unto thee with a voice of thanksgiving."*[19]

These men were delivered by the might and power of our great God as they prayed and praised Him.

Our great and mighty God answers our cry when we praise Him. He calms our storms and enables us to overcome disaster and rise above loss because we look to Him. What a wonderful Father! What a faithful God! He is always with us to help us. Through faith's words and deeds, He comes!

---

[18] Act 16:25
[19] Jon 2:9

CHAPTER 14

KEEP YOUR EYE ON THE WORD

The stumbling block to the effective operation of faith is the physical senses –seeing, hearing, feeling and taste. **In spite of our knowledge that faith works through the Word of God, we are prone to be thrown off course by our senses.** Our senses forever alert us to trauma, whether real or imagined, saying, "Do you feel that? Do you see that? Can you hear that noise?" If we listen to its voice, we are dominated by our body, not by our spirit.

From the vantage point of faith, the role of the physical body is to tell us when our faith should be active so that a problem can be eliminated. And, our faith should always be ready. This is the purpose of meditation. It keeps our spirit full of God's Word, always ready like a high-speed computer to pour the Scriptures into every situation.

As a Christian, meditation is a lifestyle. It is more than reading the Bible through; it is more than having a verse for the day; it is more than a last minute effort to meet an emergency need by claiming God's promises. **It is how we live every minute of every day.**

In years past, I was a "professional" coffee drinker. You probably wouldn't believe the number of cups of coffee I consumed every day. But, the time came, when the Word of God ministered life to me and set me on a course of freedom. By the Spirit, the apostle Paul wrote, "Some of you say, 'We can do anything we want to.' But

I tell you not everything is good for us. So I refuse to let anything have power over me."[1] These words spoke to me repeatedly and prompted me to make a change. It was a change of LIFESTYLE.

We are usually associated with our lifestyle. People think of us in conjunction with those activities that consume our time. If your neighbor loves to fish and you notice that he is not home, your first thought might be, "He is probably at the lake today." When your "sold out to exercise" friend does not answer his phone, you are sure he is at the gym. If you haven't seen your motorcycle buddies today, you would suppose they are out riding. It is their lifestyle.

In the Scriptures, we are counselled to continually meditate in God's Word.

The psalmist said that we must meditate day and night.[2] Of course, this does not mean I am reading God's Word every minute of every day. This would be impossible. But it does mean that the Word of God is a priority in my life. Daily, I read my Bible, and when the Holy Spirit prompts me to read and re-read a passage of Scripture, I obey. After all, this is not a race to the finish line. It is a rain-soaking shower that pours the water of the Word into my heart.

---

[1] 1Co 6:12 CEV
[2] Ps 1:2

When I think about meditation, it reminds me of the many hours that we worked to help our children learn the multiplication tables. We rehearsed them constantly until someone could ask, "What's six times six, and the answer, thirty-six, was automatic." Still today, I know my multiplication tables because of our studies together.

I also apply these principles of meditation – this continual rehearsal – when I study to teach. In fact, it dominates everything I do. I find myself reading the books that have blessed me over and over again. The binding on many of my books is unstable and the covers are often taped together because I use them repeatedly. But it is through this meditation that the Holy Spirit brings to my remembrance the words I need to hear again.

THE LEADERSHIP OF THE SPIRIT

Through meditation, the Holy Spirit also helps us to recognize the voice of the flesh and physical senses. Because our physical senses cannot discern the plan of God, the Holy Spirit is our guide! According to the apostle Paul:

For his Holy Spirit speaks to us deep in our hearts.[3]

[3] Rm 8:16 NLT

The Message Bible writes, "God's Spirit touches our spirit." The New Century Version declares, "The Spirit himself joins with our spirits." For this reason, we depend on the Holy Spirit to validate the testimony of the Word of God, not our physical senses.

The Scripture counsels us to:

...live by what we believe, not by what we can see.[4]

In 2 Corinthians 4:18, we read this again. It states:

While we look not at the things which are seen, but at the things which are not seen.

If we look at, or constantly consider, things that are seen, we give the physical senses credence, often using them to guide our lives. We judge our circumstances with our senses, instead of by the Word of God. If this is the case, we should not be surprised when our dilemma is not solved. **The physical senses cannot perceive the will of God.**

---

[4] 2Co 5:7 NCV

Most of us are familiar with the biblical record that tells us Peter walked on the water to Jesus. After Jesus had fed about 5,000 men, plus women and children, He told the disciples to row to the other side of the sea while He went into a mountain to pray. While they were rowing, Jesus came toward them walking on the water. Although the disciples were very afraid, Peter asked Jesus if he could walk to Him on the water, and Jesus told him to come.

Peter was walking on the water when he noticed the wind blowing violently. The Scripture records that "he saw the wind boisterous."[5] I've teased those in our classes saying, "He should have chosen a day when the wind wasn't blowing." But actually, the wind was immaterial and irrelevant.

> *It doesn't matter how calm or tempestuous the wind, you can't walk on the water.*

Yet by faith in Jesus' word, Peter was walking on the water. Then he allowed his physical senses to rule him, and with his senses in charge, he began to sink. His physical senses upended his faith.

When we trust in God's Word, we embrace the promises that God has given us, and though our

---

[5] Mt 14:30

physical senses may contradict God's report, we hold fast to the Word of the Lord.

The writer of Hebrews says:

Let us hold fast the profession of our faith without wavering; (for he is faithful that promised.)[6]

I love the terminology "hold fast." Often, I have tritely said, "If I left you in the Atlantic Ocean with a life preserver and told you I will be back to pick you up tomorrow, I would not have to tell you to hold fast." There is no doubt that I would find you clinging to the life preserver.

In like manner, we "hold fast" to the Word of God. We do not let our bodies, or any thought that does not agree with God's Word, lead us astray. **We do not let reason and logic dictate our choices.** We are not guided by pros and cons.

Instead, we "let God be true, but every man a liar."[7]

---

[6] Heb 10:23
[7] Rm 3:4

The power of the living God is greater than reason and stronger than any results we think inevitable. The Scripture proves this many times. Moses opened a pathway through the Red Sea with a rod.[8] Shadrach, Meshach, and Abed-nego stood in a fiery furnace, but they were not consumed.[9] Daniel was thrown into a lions' den, yet he was not harmed.[10] Peter was released from prison by an angel.[11] Philip was transported by the Spirit of the Lord to a new location.[12] Are any of these incidents logical? No. Are they reasonable? No. But are they God? Yes! Definitely yes!

The book of Proverbs says:

Trust in the Lord with all thine heart; and lean not unto thine own understanding. In all thy ways acknowledge him, and he shall direct thy paths.[13]

What wonderful news! **If we do NOT rely on our own intelligence or perception, God will order our**

[8] Ex 14:16
[9] Dan 3:26-27
[10] Dan 6:23
[11] Act 12:5-10
[12] Act 8:39-40
[13] Pr 3:5-6

steps.

One day, I heard someone ask, "How would you like to be at the right place at the right time?" With the leadership of our mighty God, that is exactly what will happen.

The writings of the psalmist declare that God's Word "is settled in Heaven."[14] We understand the word "settled" because we use it with our children. They may ask several times to do something that we have forbidden. Eventually, we say, "I said no and that settles it." What do we mean by that? We mean that is our final answer.

Well, the Word of God is settled! He said:

By [Jesus'] stripes ye were healed.[15]

Therefore, when our body and mind rage out of control, when they tell us we are not healed, we yield to God and His Word because that is God's final answer! **We speak His promises continually, and then we thank Him for His healing power that is working mightily in us.** We do not heed that voice that looks diligently for physical evidence and loudly declares, "I don't see anything." We have plenty of evidence!

---

[14] Ps 119:89
[15] 1Pe 2:24

Faith is "the evidence of things not seen." [16] Therefore, speak God's Word boldly! Trust in Him. He is working!

---

[16] Heb 11:1

CHAPTER 15

HONOR THE ANOINTING

I was an adult before I noticed the scriptural word "anointing." This very important, powerful word enables men to do the work of God. Men preach with the anointing. They teach by the anointing, and the offices of apostle, evangelist and prophet also depend on the anointing. This mighty manifestation from heaven also heals our bodies and minds, upending the work of Satan, who seeks to kill and destroy.

In the Old and New Testament, the word **"anointing" means to rub with oil** or smear with oil.[1] I understand this definition because Wayne and I often cook meat and vegetables on our grill, and we rub them in olive oil. Now, there is a reason for the oil that is poured on vegetables and meat, just as there is a purpose for the anointing.

The prophet Isaiah unveiled the purpose of the anointing when he said burdens are taken away and yokes are destroyed because of the anointing.[2] Jesus explained this further saying that by the anointing he would preach the gospel to the poor, the captive, and the blind.[3] He would bring healing and liberty to the brokenhearted and bruised. **By the anointing, all bondages would be broken**, including the oppression of

---

[1] H4886;G5548 Strong's
[2] Is 10:27, author's paraphrase
[3] Lk 4:18

sickness and disease.

Through these words of Jesus, we know that by the anointing men are set free from every destructive work. But we ask ourselves, "What is the anointing?"

The anointing is the supernatural provision of God given to men by the Holy Spirit.

Jesus stated this, saying:

The Spirit of the Lord is upon me, for he has anointed me.[4]

In Acts 10:38, the apostle Peter also testified to this truth when he writes:

God anointed Jesus of Nazareth with the Holy Ghost and with power.

Then he, too, revealed the work of God's powerful anointing, saying:

[4] Lk 4:18, NLT, Biblegateway.com

[Jesus] went about doing good, and healing all that were oppressed of the devil.

This bondage-breaking anointing is clearly displayed in the ministry of Jesus. As He was teaching and preaching, the multitudes followed Him, desiring to touch Him because through that touch they were healed. Their touch transferred the anointing from Jesus to them, and by that anointing, they were made whole.

The record of the woman with the issue of blood again discloses this powerful truth. She said:

If I may touch but his clothes, I shall be whole.

The Scripture declares that when she touched Him, immediately virtue (which is the power or anointing of God) went out of Jesus into her body and she was healed.[5]

This transfer of anointing can also be seen in the ministry of the apostle Paul. Special miracles were done through handkerchiefs, or aprons, that were brought

---

[5] Mk 5:25-34

from his body to the sick.[6] When Paul laid hands on these handkerchiefs, the anointing was transported from him to the handkerchief and then from the handkerchief to the sick person. Because of the anointing, the:

...diseases departed from them, and the evil spirits went out of them.[7]

In my own ministry, one year while teaching in Russia, I laid hands on a neck scarf to send to a sick child. Suddenly, there was such a tangible manifestation of God's power that our interpreter and the child's parents were visibly impacted. The moment I began to pray, the anointing leaped from my hand into the scarf like lightening. The next day, the child was well enough to attend the teaching session simply because the power of God had been transported to him through the scarf.

FAITH IN THE ANOINTING

The anointing flows like electricity or water. It flowed into the woman with the issue of blood when she touched Jesus' clothes, and it flowed into the

---

[6] Act 19:11-12 NKJV
[7] Act 19:12

multitudes when they touched the hem of His garment.[8] By their touch of faith, they received God's healing power.

At the same time, the anointing flowed into others as Jesus touched them. The leper was cleansed immediately as Jesus touched him. When Jesus touched Peter's mother-in-law, the great fever left her. He touched two blind men, and they received their sight.[9] God's powerful anointing was transferred to them through THEIR faith.

Faith is always the catalyst that transfers the healing anointing from God's servants to a diseased body. Jesus confirmed this truth in the story of the woman with the issue of blood when He said:

Daughter, they faith hath made thee whole.[10]

We witness this same reality as He spoke to the two blind men, declaring:

---

[8] Mk 5:28-30;Mt 14:35-36
[9] Mt 8:1-4,14-15;Mt 9:27-30
[10] Mk 5:34

> *According to your faith be it unto you.*[11]

Without faith, the anointing is inactive, or passive. One precious lady was prayed for many, many times without any notable results. Certainly, it is acceptable to pray for a person more than once because Jesus prayed for a blind man twice.[12] But in her case, she was prayed for so many times because she did not understand the role of faith. She expected an immediate physical manifestation, and when this did not happen, she quickly sought another touch from God. She did not know how to activate and maintain the anointing with her faith.

When hands are laid on us, we must look beyond our symptoms, knowing that we have received the power of God and that it is now working in our body. For this reason, it is often suggested we continually say, "Hands were laid on me on [a particular date], and I know the anointing is in my body working mightily." I like this confession because it helps anchor our faith.

THE ANOINTED WORD

Laying on of hands is one of the six fundamental

---

[11] Mt 9:29
[12] Mk 8:22-26

doctrines of the church.[13] It is used to transfer healing power from one person to another, but it also has other purposes. In the book of Acts, after the twelve disciples selected seven men to assist in business matters, they laid hands on them.[14] When the church at Antioch separated Barnabas and Paul for the work of God, they also laid hands on them.[15] Through the laying on of hands, all of these were commissioned to do the work of God. We see this in the Old Testament when Moses laid hands on Joshua. The Scripture records:

And Joshua the son of Nun was full of the spirit of wisdom; for Moses had laid his hands upon him." (Deu 34:9)

Now, as we consider the various purposes of the anointing, here is a vital question. Is a tangible anointing always present when hands are laid on us? Of course, the answer is no. Hands can be laid on us by any believer, with or without an anointing, simply because together we have faith in God's Word. In Mark 16:17, we read:

---

[13] Heb 6:1-2
[14] Act 6:6
[15] Act 13:2-3

And these signs shall follow them that believe.

Then it says:

They shall lay hands on the sick, and they shall recover.

This means that as a believer, we can be used of God to stand in agreement with those who are sick. What a glorious privilege to be His vessel!

Because God's Word was inspired of God, or divinely breathed, it will always heal our bodies. It is the "power of God unto salvation" [16] and, according to Strong's Exhaustive Concordance of the Bible, this salvation includes rescue, safety, deliverance, preservation, and health.[17] From this definition, we are assured that **God's great plan of redemption rescues us from sin and sickness**. Our God not only heals by a transfer of anointing, but He also "sent his word" to heal us.[18]

---

[16] Rm 1:16
[17] G4991
[18] Ps 107:20

We will recover as we believe God's anointed Word. Our body may say, "You are not healed. It isn't working." But we trust in God.

He said:

> *By whose [Jesus] stripes you were healed."[19]*

Therefore, we boldly declare our faith. "Today, according to the Word of God, I am healed. Today, God's power is working mightily in my body."

What cause for rejoicing! As the Scripture says:

> *Anyone who trusts in him will never be disappointed.[20]*

Amen!

---

[19] 1Pe 2:24
[20] Rm 10:11 NCV

SECTION 4

NO MORE OBSTACLES

For if we would judge ourselves, we should not be judged (1Co 11:31).

THE FINALE

IT'S NOT WORKING!

It's not working! This is a very familiar cry to pastors, teachers, and other ministers who pray for the sick, and understandably so. When your body aches and the symptoms of disease multiply, it is easy to become discouraged. In these moments, we often yield to the pain and agony of disease, certain that the Word of God is not working, or at least, that it is not working for us.

But according to God's Word:

> *...we walk by faith, not by sight.*[1]

In spite of our physical and mental anguish, we know God is working. Therefore, we refuse to surrender to our senses, allowing pain to steal our faith. Instead, we:

> *...hold fast the profession of our faith without wavering.*[2]

---

[1] 2Co 5:7
[2] Heb 10:23

We cannot, we must not, allow our bodies to overrule our faith and declare defeat.

We cannot give up.

One day, a friend embarked on a three-mile walk with her family. However, it wasn't very long before one of her children wanted to turn around and go home. I understand this because I've done the same thing. Once, I was walking with a friend when I decided the walk was too hard and too long, and, of course, this is Florida, so it was definitely too hot. I thought it was a good idea to surrender and go home.

Yet instead of allowing our body to continually give a negative report, encouraging us to surrender, **we must hold fast to God's Word**. We choose the report of the Lord over the report of our physical senses. Our great and mighty God "can be trusted to keep His promise."[3] Through faith and patience, we will inherit every blessing given to us in the Word of God.[4]

OUR CONFESSION

As we walk by faith in God's Word, the Scripture guides our confession. Our words acknowledge God's bountiful promises, not our distress.

---

[3] Heb 10:23 NLT
[4] Heb 6:12, author's paraphrase

The psalmist said:

Let the redeemed of the Lord say so.[5]

Then, he continually said:

Oh that men would praise the Lord for his goodness, and for his wonderful works to the children of men![6]

Certainly, it is the goodness of God that fills our words.

Our faith grows stronger when we acknowledge the promises of God's Word and talk about His goodness. However, constantly speaking about our dilemma allows the voice of our senses to dominate us and cripple our faith. It causes us to retreat in despondency and despair instead of drawing us toward the healing power of God.

Discouragement is inevitable if we look to our body for the answer. But through confession of God's promises we find victory, even when our body is not

---

[5] Ps 107:2
[6] Ps 107:8,15,21,31

instantly aware that the mighty power of heaven is hard at work. God's work begins in our spirit and then flows into our body. After teaching healing classes for years, I have found that failure to understand this important principle is a major cause of failure and loss.

Through discouragement and depression, the door of defeat and loss opens wide. When we yield to their attack, we become like a train that jumps the track before it gets to its destination. Don't do this! Stay on track! **Daily remind yourself** that the body's distress cannot prevent the Word of God from bringing full recovery. Remember:

Everything is possible for him who believes.[7]

If we hold fast to God's Word of faith, the power of God works effectively in us.

FAITH AND LOVE

Through our faith in God and His Word, we anticipate victory. But even **faith cannot rescue us if God's love is not the foundation of our behavior.** The apostle Paul shared this very important principle in Galatians 5:6 when he declared that faith works by love.

---

[7] Mk 9:23 NIV

We previously learned that "faith works," but now we must add to our knowledge that faith works through love. **If we do not obey God's New Testament command of love, faith cannot deliver us from difficulties.**

Faith and love always work together! Bitterness, jealousy, anger, hatred, selfishness, and other works of the flesh are roadblocks to faith's power.

> *Our faith can be secure and our confession sound, but if love does not rule our lives, faith is paralyzed.*

It simply cannot function.

According to the Lord Jesus Christ, we must love our neighbor as much as we love ourselves."[8] Certainly, we cannot ignore this command and expect to be healed. How can I expect God to hear my voice and answer my cry when I refuse to hear and heed the voice of His Word to love others?

The Word of God is our guide in every relationship. When we obey its command, we will not hate our enemy. Instead, we will bless them, pray for them, and do good things for them.[9] This is the instruction of the Scripture and the word given to us by our Lord Jesus. Although it seems impossible, we are not overwhelmed

---

8 Mt 22:39, author's paraphrase
9 Mt 5:44

because we know God's love dwells in our spirit, and with it, we love all men.[10] We are so grateful God equipped us for victory by giving us the key to effectively functioning faith.

JUDGE YOURSELF

When we fail to obey God's principle of love, we must judge ourselves and correct our behavior. If we do not change, our faith cannot respond to our need, and we become like a car that does not run. Nothing is more discouraging than placing your key in the ignition and getting no response.

We "judge ourselves" with the counsel of God.[11] **God's Word is the best measure and only standard of godly conduct.** By submitting to His wisdom, we can live in victory.

On the other hand, there is no doubt we are hindered when we refuse God's command. If we maintain ungodly behavior, our walk with God is crippled. We have only to look in the Scripture to prove this point. Cain killed his brother, Abel, and became a fugitive and vagabond in the earth.[12] Esau sold his birthright and failed to inherit a blessing.[13] Jonah cried out to God from the belly of a fish after he refused to

---

[10] Rm 5:5
[11] 1Co 11:31
[12] Ge 4:12
[13] Heb 12:16-17

deliver God's message to Ninevah.[14]

But there is good news. In the first epistle of John, we read:

If we confess our sins, he is faithful and just to forgive us our sins, and to cleanse us from all unrighteousness.[15]

We hear this promise again in the book of James when it says:

The prayer of faith shall save the sick, and the Lord shall raise him up; and if he hath committed sins, they shall be forgiven him.[16]

What glorious promises from the Word of God! **When we confess our sins, we can be forgiven and healed.**

Certainly, the apostle Peter knew this well. After denying our Lord three times, he bowed his head,

---

[14] Jon 1:17
[15] 1Jn 1:9
[16] Jas 5:15

weeping bitterly.[17] Yet in the book of Acts, the Holy Spirit enabled him to preach a word from God that brought three thousand souls to repentance.[18] What an amazing change! What glorious forgiveness!

Today, we carefully examine our heart and allow God to speak to us. With His Word as our guide, we walk steadily forward, always doing those things that please Him.[19] As we yield to faith and love, He orchestrates our success, and, of course, this includes healing for our body and mind. Oh, how we love Him. He is our Lord!

---

[17] Lk 22:62
[18] Act 2:41
[19] Col 1:10

ABOUT THE AUTHOR

Reverend Becky Combee has been teaching Bible principles in home and church groups for over thirty-five years. She is known for her Bible knowledge, unique humor, and atypical sketches.

Ordained in 1996 under the ministry of Pastor Reggie Scarborough of Family Worship Center in Lakeland, Florida, she ministers the Word of God in her local church, across the United States, and around the world.

Becky Combee is a native Floridian. She and her husband, Wayne, have been married for fifty years and have two children who assist them in ministry giving computer expertise, photographic skills, and office administration.

Becky and Wayne Combee are committed to the Word of God as truth and the Holy Spirit as God who reveals truth. It is their heart's desire to clearly define the Word of God to all who will hear in our world.

More information about Becky Combee Ministries, Inc. can be found at www.beckycombeeministries.com.